HAS GOD FINISHED WITH ISRAEL?

COMMENDATIONS

'The role of the Land and People of Israel has continuously been neglected by most of Christendom. It has also been said that Israel is the missing link in systematic theology. The result is that the Church has often, not only perpetrated an anti-Judaic polemic but has also failed to understand the significance of "covenant". This book contains the key to understanding God's continued purposes for both the Jewish people and the Church. Rob Richards' book is one of the most significant works written on the subject.'

Rev Canon Andrew White,
Director of International Ministry at Coventry Cathedral

'This book is a stimulating and helpful read for anyone wishing to answer the question about the Church and Jewish people. It is thorough and yet very accessible . . . it should be on the required reading list for every Christian as it deals with one of the most important issues the Church faces.'

Joseph Steinberg,
co-founder Y2000 and co-author of the Y Course.

Has God Finished with Israel?

ROB RICHARDS

WORD PUBLISHING

Milton Keynes, England

HAS GOD FINISHED WITH ISRAEL?

Previously published 1994 by Monarch Publications.

This revised edition published 2000 by Word Publishing,
a division of Word Entertainment Ltd, 9 Holdom Avenue,
Bletchley, Milton Keynes, Bucks, MK1 1QR, UK.

ISBN 1 86024 357 6

Text illustrations by Drew Snell

Biblical quotations are from the
New International Version © 1973, 1978, 1984
by the International Bible Society

Produced for Word Publishing by
Bookprint Creative Services, P.O. Box 827, BN21 3YJ, England.
Printed in Great Britain.

CONTENTS

Part II   EXPLORING AN APPLICATION

ACKNOWLEDGEMENTS

This is to thank all those who have helped me in this search, especially to Anna for all her love, and for putting up with me as I have struggled with this issue, as well as Jon, Katharine and Libby. My thanks too go to the Revd Jos Drummond, the Revd John Fieldsend, Peter Zimmermann and Les Palmer for all their work on the proof-reading stages, Drew Snell for his drawings, J. John for challenging me to continue working through issues that are raised in this book, and not least to Pat, who prayed without ceasing.

For the revised edition, my thanks go to Sue Taylor for all the typing, and especially to the Revd Michael McCrum for his thorough editorial work.

In writing this I well realise that I am drawing from the thoughts of others in various passages in this book. Having left theological college, I found that for study purposes, the wide margined NIV Bible provided a most effective way for recording brief quotes and odd comments relevant to passages of Scripture as I came across them from different sources, heard others preaching, or listened to teaching tapes. Little did I realise that one day I would be asked to write a book! I do not always record the source in these margin notes and this has been reflected in the absence of footnote references. If something is said that you believe to be original to yourself, do please accept my thanks where it has influenced me. I am very conscious of Paul's words to the Corinthian church, 'What do you have that you did not receive?' (1 Cor 4:7).

The content of the following chapters is purely a personal search over the years. It is unfinished in that there is still much that I need to rework.

FOREWORD

Today we do indeed live in interesting times. Nowhere is this more true than in the affairs of Israel and the rest of the Holy Land. Tears of joy and sadness, of hope and mourning, have been shed over Jerusalem continually since Jesus shed his tears as Son of God nearly 2,000 years ago, and there is no abatement to the crying.

Much has been written and said by Christians on the whole issue of Israel, much of it triumphant, insensitive and simplistic. This book stems the flow. It is a journey of one man, challenged I believe by God, to take a close and deep look again at the place of Israel within the purposes of God. Those who look to this book for simplistic Zionism or a vitriolic attack on Judaism will be disappointed, and rightly so. This book calls us back to Scripture, to take our Bible seriously and to search the pages of God's Word to try and understand his plans and ways. In so doing we can discover and hear from God what our role is as individuals, and more important as his Church, in proclaiming the Good News of Jesus Christ to all the people of the world.

Rob Richards' writing is honest and sincere, his approach fresh, illuminative and thought provoking. It is an important contribution to the debate over Israel and an example to be thoroughly Biblical in all our thinking and actions. We resist and ignore such a call at our peril – not only our own, but that of all the people of the world. Only when we are in step with God and his ways can we turn the curse of these interesting times into a blessing.

J. John
Chorleywood, England
November 1999

PREFACE

It might have been a picture post card. The Sea of Galilee glistened in the sunshine early one beautiful spring morning. I was sitting by the water full of expectancy, my Bible open. I had never been to Israel before and in this moment of time I was transported back 2,000 years. Here was the very water upon which Jesus walked as he demonstrated his lordship over wind and waves. At that moment on the shiny water an oil slick slowly drifted in front of me. How could that be happening, this was the *Holy* Land, there couldn't be oil slicks on Galilee? But there were! My early morning meditations were shaken as I adjusted to the fact that this was two thousand years later and times had changed. No sooner had I composed myself back into a suitable lakeside account of Jesus, than a man came up, no more than two yards on my left, and proceeded to attend to a call of nature. By now, the 'holiness' of the moment, if there had been any, had vanished and I was left with a sense that there was much that I needed to learn if I were to understand what relevance this small land had two thousand years after Jesus. Presumably those Galilean fishermen must have had the need to relieve themselves along the shores of the Lake, but why did the culture have to be so different? I mean – if in desperation, we would at least have been careful to see that no one was looking – wouldn't we?

For me a search had begun. Why did I found it so difficult to make a connection between present day Israel and Jewish people and the same land and race that were the context of Jesus' coming? Two thousand years have rolled by and today Israel is almost always in the news. Were Jewish people still the 'chosen people' and, if so for what? Would it still be relevant anyway? Why were some Christians so excited about Israel? Could a secular state be a part of God's purposes? Even though I had found Jesus as Lord and Saviour, modern Israel did not register as any more or less important than England or anywhere else in the world.

As I began to read press reports and articles relating to this subject, I was amazed to discover that close to one third of all United Nations' resolutions concern Israel, yet she is a nation of around only one twelve thousandth of the world's population! The land of Israel is about the size of Wales and is surrounded by Arab nations with a land mass equivalent to the United States of America. So why is this little nation of such notice to the world? Why does it stand out so significantly in world affairs? Why does this tiny country have the second largest press corps after the USA? More particularly, has God any part to play in all this, or has He finished with Israel? Are we seeing a human struggle for power in the Middle East that is in direct conflict with God's purposes, or is God at work through all these Middle Eastern events?

These are issues with which the author has struggled. If the answer is that God has finished with Israel, then affairs in the Middle East seem as vexing as anywhere in the world. If the answer is that God has *not* finished with Israel, then might we actually be seeing events unfolding before us, which have enormous consequences for the world?

I was soon to discover that it is impossible to speak of Israel, whether the Jewish people, the land of Israel or lifting the lid on the question of the Ten Lost Tribes (of Israel), and not be seen by some as making a political statement. The intention of the book is essentially apolitical. In that, it may not succeed.

The book seeks to answer some of these related questions, 'Does God have a continued commitment to the Jewish people and Israel?', and if so, 'What?', 'Has the Church 'replaced' Israel?' and 'If the Jewish people are 'chosen', then why?' It then seeks to see what part Israel plays in Biblical prophecy, although it is not written for those seeking a precise countdown to the Second Coming of the Lord Jesus Christ, nor is it written especially to identify current events with Biblical prophecy, as events so quickly date in the Middle East.

If you are one who likes future events to be charted out in diagrammatic form for at-a-glance understanding, you may be disappointed, although I do have a stab at a different illustration of the ongoing nature of God's revealed purposes in the Bible. For those who are looking for footnotes to qualify each statement and a lengthy bibliography, again, you will be disappointed. I realise that every verse quoted has had literary wars fought over it and perhaps literal ones too! It is impossible therefore to qualify every statement.

I adopt the thesis that all we need to know concerning God's revealed purposes for the world, the Church and for Israel are to be found within the covers of the Bible, made up of both the Hebrew Scriptures ('Old') and the 'New' Testament, neither being complete without the other. Of course, commentaries and books on Biblical topics are enormously helpful, but this book is based on the integrity of Scripture as being the prime way of understanding Scripture. It was reading books *about* Israel and Biblical prophecy that led me into such confusion. I see the difference between scholarship and revelation as crucial to understanding prophecy.

Scholarship would be the study of the writings of others on the subject and familiarising oneself with the different positions or opinions on Biblical prophecy (of which there are many), whereas revelation would be a quickening of the

Scriptures by the Holy Spirit, that brings a growing assurance and conviction on this issue.

The title of the book, *Has God Finished with Israel?* began, for me, as a hypothesis, developed into a thesis and led to a deep conviction. The book will inevitably raise serious questions and counter arguments along the way and the reader may want to note these and then go back and look at those questions in the light of later chapters.

I would refer the reader to Appendix 1, where I list the colours that I use in marking my Bible. It will help as you follow the lines of argument in understanding that I have different colours to highlight different themes in the Scriptures, and these have helped me enormously.

Luke tells us that 'the Bereans were more noble than the Thessalonians, for they received the message with great eagerness and examined the Scriptures every day to see if what Paul said was true' (Acts 17:11). So I hope that the quotations from the Bible will be the best part of the book. Please note that I have frequently added emphasis to particular aspects of these quotations by using italics.

My prayer is that God the Father will enable us to come to this subject with a freshness that only his Spirit can bring and 'that the eyes of our hearts may be enlightened in order that we may know the hope to which he has called you, the riches of his glorious inheritance in the saints' (Eph 1:18).

Part I

DISCOVERING A PRIORITY

Chapter 1

A TESTIMONY

I used to work in the City of London and, shortly after I became a committed Christian, saw a man in a rather drab brown mackintosh walking across London Bridge carrying a sandwich board. His message was 'The end of the world is nigh. Prepare to meet thy Maker!' The words were in a rather old-fashioned typeface and the man was clearly treated by the city commuters as a joke or someone who should be ignored at all costs! In that instance I recall that the seriousness of the statement on the one hand and yet the cost to the integrity of the message, not to mention the messenger on the other, created a sort of paralysis within me! I was on both sides of the divide that he had created. I remember making a mental note at the time not to find myself getting into such controversial waters! God has a sense of humour and here I am tackling a book that involves the Second Coming of Jesus Christ!

A year or two later, having completely forgotten that brief moment on London Bridge, I was given a book on the subject of the Second Coming and found it immensely inspiring. The imminence of his return gave a context to my life in this particular point in world history that I found enormously exciting. The title of the book and its author are not the point of the story. A few days after finishing the book I told a senior church leader how helpful I had found the book. His reply was very gracious, yet quietly firm, 'Oh no, ' he said, 'We don't have to believe that!' I looked at him, outwardly cool but inwardly crushed. 'We don't?', I replied, rather lamely. Now I valued the ministry of this particular church leader and was puzzled that the subject, which seemed so clear to me when reading the book was, in fact, far more problematical than I had first realised. How naïve can one be?

Looking back, I can see that, having taken what I thought was a big step forward in understanding Biblical prophecy, I promptly took two larger steps back, not just to the rather woolly understanding that I had at first, but to a distinctly doubting attitude towards the whole subject and to anyone who claimed that they knew how to interpret Biblical prophecy and what was going to happen in the future.

The prophets in the Old Testament (as I was so used to calling it) seemed so difficult to understand. Large portions failed to make sense. Yes, there were marvellous accounts of events in the life of Israel and Judah. The Psalms held precious promises. But much of the Hebrew Scriptures was a book that I did not really understand as a companion to the New Testament. Simple outline studies of Bible prophecies, I now treated with distrust, and simplistic statements about prophecy, I questioned. A sadness came upon me that here was an area of the Bible that I did not understand. It was closed to me.

In time, the answer became clear. The selection process of the Church of England decided that I should be ordained and to theological college I went, thinking that there I would find the answers to all my questions. As it turned out, I became more confused than ever, not least in seeing just how many books there were in the library on the subject.

To make matters worse, I would hear those lecturers 'qualified' in the New Testament, preface comments about the Old Testament by saying, 'I am not qualified in Old Testament studies but . . .' (and then quoting and interpreting a certain passage), and, similarly, the Old Testament lecturers would add the same caveat of their understanding of the New Testament. An inner despair deepened. Was there no one who could demonstrate a harmony between *both* Testaments? This is no indictment of those at whose feet I sat, as I claim to be no expert in *either* Testament.

After the first year and during the long, first summer holiday, my wife and I and the family went to stay in California with some friends of ours. He was an associate pastor of a large and prospering West Coast church and the pastor there had a very popular teaching ministry that included a great deal of 'end times' teaching. 'How does he know all this?', was my persistent response. Our spirits lifted as we sat and listened to his Bible teaching, but I could not get a handle on the subject of prophecy. I did not know where to start. I could not seem to make his favourite passages on the subject speak to me in the same way as they did to him.

So, on our return to England, I decided to do my college thesis on – you've guessed, the 'Second Coming'! That will clear things up, I thought. I was mistaken.

I bought the various books written by the West Coast Bible teacher and studied them along with endless others. My depression deepened when I spotted that this particular teacher, who seemed so clear on the subject, had, in one passage, actually pointed to a particular year in which he calculated that the Lord was going to return. Alarm bells rang loudly (later, the year came and went!); did not Jesus tell us that 'no-one knows about that day or hour'? (Matt 24:36).

On the subject of the Lord's coming again, the theological counsel that I was hearing was that central to His return was the answer to the question, 'Who is Israel?'. The teaching amongst those with whom I mixed appeared to me to say that the church was now 'the New Israel', as Israel had disobeyed God, broken his covenant, been forsaken by God and scattered to the four corners of the earth. So I followed that line and unearthed what I discovered were the three main views concerning his coming: so named, a-millennialism, pre-millennialism (especially dispensationalism), and post-millennialism. Bright sparks would add the pan-millennialism viewpoint that everything would 'pan out' all right in the end.

In summarising my position at the conclusion of my thesis, I chose the prevailing line that the church was now 'Israel' and I could take the promises made to Israel and transfer them to the church. But all the while, I was struggling with such widely differing viewpoints. How could men and women of good faith find themselves at such variance? My faith in ever finding the hope of which the prophets spoke seemed as far away as ever. I realised that in writing and finally presenting my thesis, I was merely recording the views of others.

I was ordained and served my curacy, aware that I was agnostic about the whole subject of the return of Jesus Christ and the place of Israel in God's purposes. I was unable to preach about it with any conviction and knew that it was probably not possible to give the subject as much study time as I had at college. I wondered why I could not feel comfortable with those who had such certainty about the Coming of Jesus and at the same time, I continued to experience a sense of bereavement that I still remained so unclear on the subject.

A tape of a sermon

In 1982, I was being driven to a deanery chapter meeting by my vicar. We talked nineteen to the dozen about parish issues most of the way there. He had switched on a tape of a sermon about Israel and the Jewish people, although neither of us was particularly listening to it. But as we drove to the meeting with the tape playing in the background, a thought began to come to my mind related to this whole question of an integrated understanding of Scripture and that was quite simply the phrase 'Israel is Israel is Israel!'. It seemed such an odd phrase.

The deanery meeting was not particularly memorable, but the next morning as I happened to turn to the Old Testament, it came alive in a totally new way. It was as though I had never seen the words directed so clearly to the people of Israel.

I had always found the blood and guts of the Old Testament difficult to take, but now I found myself weeping over the passages of judgments and failings of the people of Israel and then equally found joy in my spirit at the passages of restoration. I did not know how to explain the change in my understanding. It was such a dramatic new perspective of Scripture and certainly did not seem to me to connect with parish ministry, particularly as a curate in training.

Almost immediately I started to worry that I might land up being, as I had uncaringly labelled certain others, an Israel freak, but a conviction was developing that I did not know how to explain.

I do remember in those early days of discovery, preaching at an evening service on the Anglican lectionary theme for that Sunday: 'The Remnant of Israel'. It was as I was saying goodbye to people at the door afterwards that I was nearly spat on by one woman, as the words 'Zionism' hissed from her lips as she passed by me. I was shocked, and it made me go back to study again the passages that had so come alive and the priority in Scripture that I was beginning to see. I do not recall preaching again on the subject for years. Surely I had seen this incorrectly and needed much more time to understand what God was saying about Israel and prophecy.

It was around this time that I began to colour themes in my Bible. In Appendix 1, I have outlined the colour codes that I have found useful and would recommend with all my heart that the reader considers this as an aid to appreciating the major themes and consistency and integrity of Scripture. It is so easy to forget a certain slant in a passage from the Bible, a truth, a doctrine, a pattern or recurrence of what has been said before. Gradually, as the different colours started to highlight different themes, it became so much easier, through the different colours, to pick up again on passages of Scripture thereafter and not lose the understanding gained in previous readings. I leave the idea with you to investigate further.

Parish life was enormously busy and there was little time to read up on this subject, but the Bible kept encouraging me to discern the wonderful plan of salvation and restoration for the ethnic people of Israel even though it appeared irrelevant amongst my fellow clergy and almost all the different congregations among whom I worked.

Like Paul after his experience on the road to Damascus, who then spent a period of time in the wilderness (Gal 1:17), I realised that on this subject, I was in the wilderness too and, again like Paul, I did not confer with the leaders about this particular interest in prophecy and the place of Israel.

It is that journey, an ever increasing personal conviction, fuelled literally every time I opened my Bible, that I share with you in the following chapters.

Chapter 2

A PRIORITY REVEALED IN SCRIPTURE

No sooner had I started to read the Bible with that phrase 'Israel is Israel is Israel!' resonating in my spirit than a priority in the Bible that I had never seen before revealed itself, summed up in Paul's words in Romans 1:16, 'The gospel . . . is the power of God for the salvation of everyone who believes: *first* for the Jew, then for the Gentile'. I did not know that the verse even existed. You know how you could almost swear that a particular verse was not in the Bible the last time you read a passage. Paul was saying, '*first for the Jew*, then for the Gentile'.

It was as though a huge penny had dropped, an aspect of God's purposes that I had never seen. Obviously I knew intellectually that the Scriptures were written mainly by Jewish writers. So, in that sense, God had *first* chosen the Jews to reveal who he is. Luke was the only probable exception and was almost certainly a Gentile. Yet presumably he must have had converted to Judaism (as a proselyte), indicated by the fact that he shared fellowship and meals with the Apostles. Somehow it had never registered that the writers were so thoroughly Jewish.

The whole Bible began to open up in an entirely new way. From Genesis onwards, God's priority in terms of sheer weight of revelation began to reinforce this sense of priority. Thirty-six books in the Old Testament (or Hebrew Scriptures), unfolding the history of the Children of (Jacob) Israel! A mere two chapters on Creation and nine chapters on the first 2,000 years of history as recorded in the Bible, in contrast with fourteen chapters on the life of one man Abraham (the first Hebrew) and then 903 chapters focused principally on Israel, and virtually all of it written in Hebrew. That is 78% of the entire Biblical writings, quite apart from adding all the Old Testament quotations, or allusions to it found in the New Testament. How had I never seen that priority to Israel as particularly relevant?

In the gospels

My past experiences, however, had led me to mistrust what I would call proof texts about Israel's future and certainly charts that laid out Biblical events from Genesis to Revelation. As a Christian I believed that Christ had fulfilled the Old Covenant and so it had to be a conviction from the New Testament that would convince me that there still was such a priority to Israel and the gospel was 'first for the Jew'.

I began to check out this new found thesis beginning with Matthew's gospel. How else can one explain why the genealogy in Matthew chapter 1 and the Hebrew ancestry of the Jewish Messiah, descended from David and Abraham (1:1, 17), should become fascinating? I had usually skipped the first sixteen verses. A whole new world began to open up. Let me explain.

I saw in the gospels a priority in Jesus' life that I had never seen before. It was to his people, Israel. John records, 'He came to that which was his own' (or to his own people, Jn 1:11). He was born into a Jewish family, of the house of David. His Hebrew ancestry clearly recorded (in Matthew 1 and Luke 3), born of a Jewish virgin mother, whose Jewish name was Miriam (Lk 1:27). Paul writes, 'When the time had fully come, God sent his Son, born of a woman, born under law, to redeem those under law . . .' (Gal 4:4). He was brought up in a Jewish home. All his relatives were Jewish, Elizabeth and John the Baptist

(Lk 1:5, 57–61) as well as the brothers and sisters in his earthly family (Mk 6:3.). He lived, apart from his flight to Egypt as a child, in "the land of Israel" (Matt 2:21).

I spotted that John the Baptist, who came to herald the coming of the Messiah, in stating the purpose of his ministry, said, 'I myself did not know him, but the reason I came baptising with water was that he might be revealed to *Israel*' (Jn 1:31). Jesus did not come to a new ethnic group of people, or even a different land and nation. He was sent to reach the same ethnic people that made up so much of the Old Testament.

In one sense, it was all so obvious, but I had never seen the Jewishness of it all. To be honest it was rather scary. I was aware of a fear that it was all *too* Jewish for me, too unknown. This was such new ground. Did this have any relevance now to a twentieth century Gentile Christian, or was I altogether on a wrong track? To think that *my* Saviour was in fact so very Jewish and from such another culture.

But a course had been set, a challenge laid down. I simply *had* to keep following this through even if I did not really want to.

It is again saying the obvious, but Jesus was born into an observant Jewish home. I read and re-read Luke chapter 2 and he emphasises this observance. Jesus was circumcised on the eighth day according to the Law of Moses. (Lk 2:21, a cross reference to Gen 17:12). In the very next verse we are told that Joseph and Mary consecrated Jesus to the Lord (Lk 2:22–24) and offered a sacrifice as commanded in the law of Moses (Ex 13:2, 12).

By now I was found myself wanting to read what the specific laws said and to wonder that the Son of God should 'come in the flesh' (1 Jn 4:2) in the person of Jesus of Nazareth in the Land of Israel as John records with such power in his gospel introduction, 'The Word became flesh and made his dwelling among us' (Jn 1:14).

Luke continues, 'Every year his parents went to Jerusalem for the Feast of the Passover' (Lk 2:41) and reminds us that Jesus was regular at the synagogue (Lk 4:16). He was asked to read from the Hebrew Scriptures (Lk 4:17).

Looking back at my Christian life, I had frequently prayed that I would know the Lord better and now I was realising that here might be an answer to that prayer. It was as though hundreds of years had covered a wonderful portrait of him in his first century setting with layers of Western thinking that had masked this aspect of his humanity. I began to consider that he would even have looked Jewish! You may remember that the woman at Jacob's well in John Chapter 4 recognised Jesus as a Jew when she says (in Jn 4:9), 'You are a Jew and I am a Samaritan woman. How can you ask me for a drink? (For Jews do not associate with Samaritans)'. Search as I may, I could not find the verse where Jesus says to her 'Hello, I am a Jew!' The Samaritan woman, out at midday to fetch water, could *see* that he was a Jew. What an impression the stained glass windows depicting Jesus had been to me as a youngster, but in those he certainly did not look Jewish.

Jesus spent much of his time teaching and was also recognisably a Jewish teacher of the law. He was called 'teacher' by Nicodemus (Jn 3:2), a member of the ruling Sanhedrin. He was frequently addressed as 'Rabbi' (see John 1:38, 49; 3:2, 26; 6:25) and almost certainly dressed as an observant Jewish Rabbi of the day would be expected to dress, with the tassels of his prayer shawl showing as prescribed in Numbers 15:37,38. Interestingly, the central tassel on each corner was to be coloured blue and signified strength. It is purely conjecture, but we are told that the 'woman who had been subject to bleeding for twelve years', tried to touch his clothes (Mark 5:27) or his garment (most other translations). It adds nuance to the Scripture, 'At once Jesus realised that power had gone out from him' (5:30). Perhaps that blue tassel was the very strand that the woman was trying to reach and touch.

The point was that here was a new world to explore, the

aspect of the Jewishness of Jesus, seeing him as an observant Jew, a Jewish rabbi, looking Jewish and dressing as a Jewish teacher of the Law would be expected to dress.

Pilate knew he was a Jew. 'Am I a Jew?', he asked Jesus at his mock trial. 'It was your people and your chief priests who handed you over to me' (Jn 18:35). How staggering that God in person, should be standing in front of the Roman Governor and yet be Jewish – yes, fully God and yet fully man.

You may think that I am labouring this, but it was not just the Jewishness of Jesus that struck me with such force. It was Jesus' attitude to his own people Israel that persuaded me that there was a focus revealed in Scripture that was hugely significant.

He had called twelve to be with him. All the disciples whom he called were Jewish. What a bunch, and what an adjustment I had to make when merely discovering all their Jewish names for the first time. Jesus, whose name is Yeshua (meaning "Salvation") Ha Mashiach (The Messiah). There was Shimon, whom Jesus renamed Kefar, and Andrew, Ya'akov Ben Zavdai and Yochanan, Philip Bar-talmai, T'oma and Mattityahu, Ya'akov Bar-Chalfai and Taddai, Shimon the Zealot and Yhedua from K'riot (Matt 10:2–4. David Stern, *Jewish New Testament,* Jewish New Testament Publications, 78 Manahat, 96901 Jerusalem: 1989). Where were the familiar Anglicised names of Simon Peter, James and John? Imagine, years later, the shock that greeted me at a rather well-heeled Church of St James at my saying that their patron saint was St Ya'akov.

How amazing that with so much of his teaching set in the context of a meal, there is no reference that I can find to his eating in a Gentile home. Indeed Peter tells us that 'it is against our law for a Jew to associate with a Gentile or visit him' (Acts 10:28) and being observant, Jesus would not have done so either. How could he otherwise stand before the Pharisees and say, quite openly, 'Can any of you prove me guilty of sin?' (Jn 8:46).

I have absolutely no doubt that in the large crowds that came out to hear Jesus speak, there would have been hundreds of Gentiles. Was not Galilee also referred to as 'Galilee of the Gentiles' (Matt 4:15, Isa 9:1)? Yet it came as a real surprise to discover only four recorded conversations that Jesus had with individual Gentiles apart from his trials before Pilate. The reader may want to check this out first. As far as I could see, he spoke to the Roman centurion whose servant he healed, the Samaritan woman at the well of Sychar, the Samaritan leper and the Canaanite mother. I noted that not only did all his replies point to himself but included his focus on Israel.

The Roman centurion recognised Jesus' authority, 'Lord . . . I myself am a man under authority', to which Jesus replied, 'I have not found anyone in Israel with such great faith' (Matt 8:8–10). To the woman at the well, mentioned earlier, he said, 'Salvation is from the Jews' (Jn 4:22). To the leper whom he had healed and who returned to give thanks, he said, 'Was no-one found to return and give praise to God except this foreigner?' (Lk 17:18).

However, what really amazed me was his reply to the Canaanite woman, whose daughter was afflicted by a demon. One would have thought that she was well within her rights to plead to the Lord for him to heal her afflicted daughter. 'Lord, Son of David, have mercy on me! My daughter is suffering terribly from demon-possession.' It seems rather unfair that the Lord should ignore her, 'Jesus did not answer a word', and that she should be dismissed by the disciples, 'Send her away, for she keeps crying out after us.' But it was Jesus' statement to the twelve as to why he had been silent to her appeal that so struck me, 'I was sent *only to the lost sheep of Israel*' (Matt 15:22–24).

Might I ask if you had previously seen this focus, 'I was sent only to the lost sheep of Israel'? Yes, they had to repent. Yes, they had to believe (Mk 1:15). There was no other gospel. He was the gospel message in person. But Israel was his first priority. He was sent *first* to proclaim the gospel to them! Yet even with this emphasis, Jesus sees such faith in this troubled woman as Matthew records, 'And her daughter was healed from that very hour' (15:28). But the point was the clarity of Jesus' stated priority.

Perhaps you know the experience when the adrenaline begins to pump and an energy is released that makes you feel a drive that is exhilarating. I could not be more motivated to test this further. Jesus said 'I . . . speak just what the Father has taught me' (John 8:28) and 'I have obeyed my Father's commands' (Jn 15:10) and, again, 'So whatever I say is just what the Father has told me to say' (Jn 12:50). That meant that God the Father, the God of Abraham, Isaac and Jacob and the God and Father of our Lord Jesus Christ was *first* revealing himself to his covenant people and that was what Jesus *first* came to do.

This priority of Jesus to reach his own people first threw new light on Jesus' 'Great Commission' recorded at the end of Matthew and Luke. During his ministry in Galilee, Jesus had sent his disciples, saying 'Do not go among the Gentiles, or enter any town of the Samaritans. Go rather to the lost sheep of Israel' (Matt 10:5, 6.), an echo of his own words to the Canaanite woman. What he was doing, *they* were to do. So, following his resurrection appearance at which he gave them the Great Commission, he states they were 'to obey everything I have commanded you' (Matt 28:20). In Luke, he is more specific: 'and repentance and forgiveness of sins will be preached in his name to all nations, *beginning at Jerusalem*' (Lk 24:47). In Acts, before leaving his disciples, he again confirmed where they were to *start* in terms of mission, '. . . And you will be my witnesses in Jerusalem, and in all Judea and Samaria, and to the ends of the earth' (Acts 1:8). It followed to me that in the same way that Jesus had gone first to his people the Jews, and just as he had sent his disciples first to their fellow Jews, so they were to teach the disciples whom they would train in the gospel to do likewise.

Even thinking such thoughts challenged my hitherto understanding that the Great Commission was unconditionally universal. You can see what an enormous re-focus this was requiring of my understanding of the gospels.

I have already said that by now I was colouring Bible passages and marking, in green, things related to the Hebrew/Israel issues in Scripture (See Appendix 1 for the author's suggested use of colours), so the Jewishness of the gospels began to make itself colourfully clear. But in truth I must say that I frequently heard a whisper from somewhere just behind me, 'Yes, but, you have forgotten . . .' and then a verse would come to mind that seemed to contradict everything that I was considering.

Gradually, I found myself having to tackle head on the very 'Yes, but!' Scriptures that had formulated my thinking concerning the Church and Israel in the first place, dealing with them one by one and so reviewing my interpretation.

King of the Jews

Perhaps the most convincing factor, having seen the focus on his people Israel, was Jesus' title, 'King of the Jews'.

It was announced at his birth that Jesus would be a king, as the angel Gabriel had said to Mary, 'The Lord God will give him the throne of his father David and he will reign over the house of Jacob for ever; his kingdom will never end' (Lk 1:32–33). The wise men from the East enquire, 'Where is the one who has been born king of the Jews?' (Matt 2:2). But somehow the announcement and question had got parcelled up with the 'Christmas story', endless carol services, mince pies, too much turkey and television.

That the gospel writers claim that he would be king at birth was something that I had never really followed through seriously. Nathanael recognised Jesus as 'the King of Israel' (Jn 1:49). Following the feeding of the 5,000, John recalls that the people perceived that he was the coming king, for his commentary says, 'Jesus, knowing that they intended to come and make him king by force, withdrew again to a mountain by himself' (Jn 6:15). When Jesus rode into Jerusalem on a donkey, it was as the foretold coming king, for Matthew and John (in Matt 21:5 and Jn 12:15) both recall the words of Zechariah (9:9), 'Rejoice greatly, O daughter of Zion! . . . See, your king comes to you . . . gentle and riding on a donkey'.

It was as king of the Jews that he was tried by Pilate. Matthew records, 'Meanwhile, Jesus stood before the governor, and the governor asked Him, 'Are you the king of the Jews?' (Matt 27:11). I had always been persuaded that his reply in the AV, 'Thou sayest', meant more like, 'That's your idea' or quite simply 'That's what you think!'. However, the interpretation of Jesus' reply in the NIV could not be clearer, 'Yes, it is as you say' (Matt 27:11, Mk 15:2, Lk 23:3). The Amplified Bible puts his reply as 'You have stated (the fact)', whereas J.B.Phillips and the The Living Bible merely give Jesus' reply as the simple statement, 'Yes'.

Actually, when I checked out Jesus' similar reply to Judas' question at the Last Supper, 'Surely not I, Rabbi?', I should have realised that his words 'Thou hast said' (Matt 26:25 AV), had to be clearer than a rather vague, 'The words are yours' (translated, 'Yes, it is you' NIV).

It was as king that he was mocked by the soldiers, 'Hail, king of the Jews!' (Matt 27:28–30.). It was as king that he was presented to the people, 'Here is your king,' Pilate said to the Jews (John 19:14). He was crucified with that inscription, 'Above his head they placed the written charge against him: THIS IS JESUS, THE KING OF THE JEWS' (Matt 27:37). Hanging on the cross, Jesus was mocked by the religious leaders, 'He saved others . . . He's the King of Israel! Let him come down from the cross and we will believe in him!' (Matt 27:42).

Consider this. At what point does he abdicate as king of Israel? Certainly he is 'KING OF KINGS AND LORD OF LORDS' (Rev 19:16) and, as Hebrews quotes, referring to Jesus, 'Your throne, O God, will last for ever and ever, and righteousness will be the sceptre of your kingdom' (Heb 1:8, quoting Ps 45:6). But does he give up his kingship of Israel? How could he? He is King of Kings, King of Israel, and *still* King of the Jews! Back I had to go to the announcement of his birth by the angel Gabriel, 'The Lord God will give him the throne of his father David and he will reign over the house of Jacob for ever; his kingdom will never end' (Lk 1:32–33).

King of the Jews and a kingdom that will never end; oh, how much this stretched my thinking. Like Mary, I could but ponder these things in my heart (Lk 2:19b). Was this the clue that there would be a future kingship, rule and reign with which I had not yet been able to come to grips? I was happy to take Isaiah 9:6, 'For to us a child is born . . .' as speaking of Jesus coming as a child (I had presumed the promised child was for us Gentiles and now saw that it was a promise to Israel!), but why did I struggle with the next verse (9:7), 'Of the increase of his government and peace there will be no end. He will reign on David's throne and over his kingdom, establishing it and upholding it with justice and righteousness from that time on and for ever.'? The only concept in which I could really believe was of a spiritual rule and reign of the risen Jesus Christ. This seemed to challenge that and perhaps threw new light on the disciples' last question to Jesus, 'Lord, are you at this time going to restore the kingdom to Israel?' (Acts 1:6). They recognised that he was the king of Israel and that the kingdom, in their worldview, had not been restored.

Jesus' reply was far less ambivalent given this priority and commitment to the lost sheep of the house of Israel. As the risen king of Israel and king of the Jews, he could easily have given a direct, 'No!', or a more gentle, 'How foolish you are, and how slow of heart . . .' as he does on the road to Emmaus, (Lk 24:25), or even, 'You are in error because you do not know the Scriptures . . .', as he does to the Sadducees when they enquire about the resurrection – in which they did not believe

(Matt 22:23,29). But, at the risk of enormous misunderstanding, he leaves them with the reply, 'It is not for you to know the times or dates the Father *has set* [in other words, has already set], by his own authority' (Acts 1:7). My assumption had always been that their question was wrong, but Jesus' reply, taken at face value implies that he accepts their assumption that he *will* restore the kingdom, but points out that it is the *timing* that is not theirs to know. Had he not already told them, 'I tell you the truth, at the renewal of all things, when the Son of Man sits on his glorious throne, you who have followed me will also sit on twelve thrones, judging the twelve tribes of Israel' (Matt 19:28)? Had he not taught them to pray, 'Your kingdom come . . . on earth as it is in heaven' (Matt 6:10)? Clearly that answer was not sufficient to prevent them from causing 'trouble all over the world . . . defying Caesar's decrees, saying that there is another king, one called Jesus' (Acts 17:6–7).

But I wasn't ready to swallow this yet. The whole concept of Jesus ruling on the throne of David asked too much of my understanding of what was meant by the term 'the kingdom of God'.

Jesus wept as he approached Jerusalem (Lk 19:41), such was his heart for his own people. Then, those few days later, as he hung on the cross, with such a priority in his ministry to the people of Israel, with his mother and his disciple John at the foot of his cross, with the Judean leaders of Israel railing at him, I wonder if he did not primarily address Israel with the words, 'Father forgive them, for they do not know what they are doing'? (Luke 23:34). I had seen that as addressed directly to the Roman soldiers and through them to the world and therefore to me. I still believe that here are the words that make forgiveness possible, through this prayer from the cross, for all those who receive God's pardon in true repentance and so are freed from the penalty of sin. I now saw his heart broken for his own people and yet saw him as being still a 'full, perfect, and sufficient sacrifice, oblation and satisfaction, for the sins of the whole world' (as the Book of Common Prayer puts it). I as a Gentile am still able to enter into the New Covenant of forgiveness and grace.

The people had cried, 'Let his blood be on us and on our children' (Matt 27:25). His cry was 'Father, forgive them, for they do not know what they are doing'. Is there *any* prayer of Jesus that his Father does not answer?!

Summary

From the thought sown as a result of hearing a tape, that 'Israel is Israel is Israel!', I discovered that the Scriptures have come to us from Israel. Jesus' priority in his earthly ministry was first to Israel. He was Jewish. His faithful observance of the Law, his focus on the 'lost sheep of the house of Israel' and his kingship had all opened the door of a new world that yet demanded far more exploration and understanding. What *was* clear was that, for me, Jesus had not finished with Israel in his earthly ministry. Far from it. Indeed, the opposite: he had made Israel the focus of his mission.

Chapter 3

RESURRECTION AND THE EARLY CHURCH

The greatest event recorded in the Bible is probably the resurrection of the Lord Jesus Christ. Yes, Creation is the most staggering event, but because of the Fall of man it becomes a great sadness (Gen 6:6). The Resurrection was the proof that God in Jesus Christ had conquered sin and death and was Lord (Rom 1:4). But as far as I could see, it was witnessed during those forty days only by Jews (Acts 1:3). As Peter proclaims to the household of Cornelius those years later, 'He was not seen by all the people, but by witnesses whom God had already chosen – by us who ate and drank with him after he rose from the dead' (Acts 10:41). You would have thought a quick visit to Pontius Pilate would have made quite an impression.

Paul lists those to whom Jesus appears during that forty day period, 'to Peter . . . the Twelve. After that, he appeared to more than five hundred of the brothers at the same time, most of whom are still living, though some have fallen asleep. Then . . . to James, then to all the apostles, and last of all . . . to me' (1 Cor 15:5–8).

In not one single instance is a resurrection appearance recorded as being with Gentiles. Surely there had to be one or two Gentiles amongst the 'five hundred of the brothers at the same time' (1 Cor 15:6)? But they could not be Jewish and

Gentile 'brothers' in Christ, for by that time, no Gentile is recorded as having accepted the Messiah, and Paul would not call unbelieving Gentiles 'brothers' in any other sense.

More amazing than that was the concept that the resurrected Lord Jesus Christ was *still* the Jewish Jesus of Nazareth! Paul says in his introductory greeting to the church at Rome, 'regarding his Son, who as to his human nature was a descendant of David, and who through the Spirit of holiness was declared with power to be the Son of God by his resurrection from the dead' (Rom 1:3–4). He has taken human nature, through death and resurrection into heaven itself and there, described by John in Revelation as 'the Lion of the tribe of Judah, the Root of David' (Rev 5:5), sits at God's right hand as our great high priest interceding for us (Heb 4:14; 7:25).

I have often thought how wonderful it will be to meet Moses, David and Daniel, Peter and Paul. Because of the hope of the resurrection, I am expecting to see them as the great Hebrew saints that they are, just as I expect to see the 'great multitude that no one could count, from every nation, tribe, people and language, standing before the throne and in front of the Lamb' (Rev 7:9). How much more wonderful to behold the one 'who as to his human nature was a descendant of David' (Rom 1:3), who is the king who 'will reign over the house of Jacob for ever' and whose 'kingdom will never end' (Lk 1:33).

So, was this priority of Jesus, 'first for the Jew' to be in the gospels only? What of the book of Acts?

In the book of Acts

On the Mount of Olives, how awe inspiring it must have been to see Jesus ascend into heaven. It was the next most important theological event after the resurrection, yet his ascension was only witnessed by Jews, 'Men of Galilee . . . why do you stand here looking into the sky . . .?' (Acts 1:11).

In Acts 1 we find the 120 that made up the Early Church were *entirely* Jewish. Luke lists the Eleven for us and we have already seen their Hebrew names. From the problems that Peter had in Acts 10 when he was called by the Holy Spirit to speak to Gentiles about the risen Lord Jesus, we *know* that they were all Jewish (Acts 1:15). We will look at that later.

In Acts chapter 2:1 and following, when the Holy Spirit came, it was only upon these Galilean Jewish believers. 'Are not all these men who are speaking Galileans?' (Acts 2:7). Luke is equally specific that it was the Festival of Pentecost that was the setting of his coming, 'When the day of Pentecost was fully come' (Acts 2:1 AV). I have been greatly blessed by the renewal movement within the Church but I had never connected the outpouring of the Holy Spirit with one of 'the Lord's appointed feasts' (Lev 23:4) given to Israel. Jesus had said in the Sermon on the Mount, 'Do not think that I have come to *abolish* the Law or the Prophets; I have not come to abolish them but to fulfil them' (Matt 5:17). I had always seen his fulfilling the Feast of Passover by being the Lamb of God, but here was *another* festival prescribed in the Law, that the Lord fulfils in sending the Holy Spirit. This meant that God's calendar, as it were, was Israel's cycle of festivals and not a *Gentile* calendar. Dwell on that for a moment. As one ordained in the Church of England I was being made to start asking the unaskable. Had we produced a Church calendar that had deliberately replaced the Biblical calendar?

The thought kept pressing me that if I were able to demonstrate to myself that there was clear teaching in the New Testament that the priority to Israel had terminated in favour of the Church, then I could get back to being a 'normal' Church of England minister, without a hidden preoccupation that was bursting to come out.

But back to my study of Pentecost. I had always supposed that the disciples were all gathered in the upper room on the day of Pentecost, as suggested by Acts 1:12, 13, 'Then they [the Eleven] returned to Jerusalem from the hill called the Mount of

Olives . . .When they arrived, they went upstairs to the room where they were staying'. In that upper room they were joined by 'the women and Mary the mother of Jesus, and with his brothers' (1:14). The meeting with the 120 (described in the very next verse) to select an apostle to replace Judas Iscariot, takes place elsewhere. We are not told where, but I suspected that upper rooms in Jerusalem did not hold 120 in those days!

Acts 2:1–2 records, 'When the day of Pentecost came, they were all together in one place. Suddenly a sound like the blowing of a violent wind came from heaven and filled the whole house where they were sitting'. Pentecost was a pilgrimage festival at which observant Jews went up to Jerusalem to the temple. It was to be 'a sacred assembly' (Num 28:26). Note that they were all sitting. The Holy Spirit filled the 'whole house' and I had therefore presupposed it must have been just that: someone's house, but Jesus had called the temple 'my *house*' (Matt 21:13). Where else in Jerusalem would there have been a courtyard to hold 3,000 (Acts 2:41)? Indeed, allowing for a response to Peter's sermon of, say, 10%, (a fair response in terms of evangelism), that would mean at least 30,000 had been outside my (supposed) upper room. Jerusalem is described as 'a city that is closely compacted together' (Ps 122:3). It was dawning on me that there simply were not streets that held large numbers of people. There was only one place that could hold those sorts of numbers and that was in the temple and its precincts. Had not Luke reminded us that following Jesus' ascension into heaven, 'they stayed continually at the temple, praising God' (Lk 24:53)? How much more so on the day of the Festival of Pentecost (or Shavuot).

Furthermore, as I read on, the Holy Spirit came only upon 'God-fearing Jews from every nation under heaven' (2:5). Where else could the 3,000 who accepted Peter's message be baptised (2:41) except in the baptismal baths (Mikvahs) on the south side of the temple? Archaeological digs have unearthed those, and I am told that a crowd that large could be baptised there in about fifteen minutes.

Peter explains the phenomena of the coming of the Spirit and addresses his hearers, 'Fellow Jews . . .' (2:14). It was Jewish people who were the firstfruits of the harvest, just as Pentecost was also known as The Feast of Weeks or firstfruits (Ex 34:22) and Israel is described as 'holy to the Lord, the firstfruits of his harvest' (Jer 2:3).

So it was on one of Israel's three great pilgrimage festivals, and still a Jewish feast, a festival that meant very little to me and one that I had written off as being 'Old Testament' that the Holy Spirit came. It troubled me that I still found all this rather too revolutionary. Yes, the Church can give great praise for the sending of the Holy Spirit, but I, for one, had totally missed the Jewish context of his coming in the first place!

In Peter's second sermon, following the healing of the crippled beggar at the temple gate called Beautiful, he summarised the Lord's purpose by saying that Jesus, came '*first* to you to bless you [Israel] by turning each of you from your wicked ways' (Acts 3:26). To the Sanhedrin, following the arrest of Peter and the other apostles, and speaking of Jesus, he said, 'God exalted him to his own right hand as Prince and Saviour that he might give repentance and forgiveness of sins to Israel' (Acts 5:31). All the time, the priority of 'first for the Jew' seemed to be holding.

Jerusalem, Judea, Samaria . . .

As Jesus had said, the gospel would go to Jerusalem and Judea and Samaria. The mission to the ends of the earth was widening. I had a problem here! Were the Samaritans Israelites, Jews or Gentiles? The Samaritans had intermarried during the exile and were despised by the Jews, who did not associate with them, though Jesus did (Jn 4:9).

According to Luke the historian, up to Acts 10 the disciples went *only* to the Jews. He writes, 'Now those who had been scattered by the persecution in connection with Stephen travelled as far as Phoenicia, Cyprus and Antioch, telling the message *only to Jews'* (Acts 11:19). There need be no clash here with Acts 8, when, speaking of the same persecution, he had written, 'those who had been scattered preached the word wherever they went. Philip went down to a city in Samaria and proclaimed the Christ there' (8:4–5). Had Luke made a mistake? Did Philip spearhead the first Gentile outreach so out of step with the thinking of the apostles? He was Jewish, and Peter stated in 10:28, 'it is against our law for a Jew to associate with a Gentile or visit him.'

The apostles must now have seen the Samaritans as distant relatives, or part of the lost sheep of the house of Israel. How else does one explain the objection of the apostles in Jerusalem at hearing about Cornelius (Acts 11:18), if Gentiles had already come to faith in Samaria?

What otherwise was I to make of Simon the sorcerer? Was the clue his name, in Hebrew, Shim'on, as was Simon Peter's, and how could Peter and John pray with those in Samaria who had accepted the word of God that they might receive the Holy Spirit (8:15), if it 'is against our law for a Jew to associate with a Gentile or visit him' (10:28)? Certainly, in the light of the criticism Peter gets from the apostles in Acts 11:1–3, 'You went into the house of uncircumcised men and ate with them', it seemed to me unlikely that the apostles in Jerusalem would send Peter and John to Gentiles in Samaria, here in Acts 8.

By now I was putting 'problem passages' to one side and every now and then going back to them to see if I was getting any more light on them.

The incident with the Ethiopian is fascinating too, but still a problem. Here was a black man and a eunuch. He had 'gone to Jerusalem to worship' (Acts 8:27), so he was a God-fearing man. He even owned a scroll of the prophet Isaiah, and they must have been expensive! The connection of Ethiopia with Israel went back to the visit of the Queen of Sheba to King Solomon in 1 Kings 10. The *Encyclopedia Judaica*, 6:1143 points out that 'Ethiopian chronicles show that Judaism was widespead before the conversion to Christianity of the Axum dynasty during the fourth century' (AD or CE- Common Era). Was this man too a proselyte to Judaism, one who would have been forbidden, as a eunuch, to join the assembly in the Temple (Dt 23:1)? (David Stern, *Jewish New Testament Commentary*, Jewish New Testament Publications: 1992, p 250.) Again, would Philip have gone to a Gentile in opposition to the apostles in Jerusalem and against Peter's declared position concerning Gentiles?

These questions were not substantial enough for me to say that here, at last, is where God ceases to demonstrate through the apostles' ministry, the priority 'first for the Jew'.

Saul

The next major section of the book of Acts concerns Saul, or Rabbi Sha'ul. Following the events of his conversion, Saul 'at once . . . began to preach in the synagogues' (Acts 9:20). Although he was called to be the apostle to the Gentiles (Rom 11:13), Saul too went *first* to the Jews. Ananias had been told, 'Go! This man is my chosen instrument to carry my name before the Gentiles and their kings *and before the people of Israel*' (Acts 9:15). We will see how seriously Paul took that latter part of his commission. To think that London's great Cathedral, St Paul's, was named after a Jewish Rabbi. My world was being turned upside down.

It is at least ten years and perhaps as many as fourteen years after the resurrection and ascension of Jesus before we reach Acts 10 and the first recorded conversion of a Gentile. Ten or more years during which time the church was still *entirely* Jewish, a group within Judaism, meeting in synagogues and the temple. The clue to this time period is in Acts 12:1 'It was about this time that King Herod . . .', and if you read on, the same Herod dies an unfortunate death in his coastal resort fortress town of Caesarea (12:23). Luke the historian wants us to link this period of activity in the Church to an historical date. Herod died in AD 44 (*New Bible Dictionary*, IVP). Jesus died and rose again in, well, it depends what book you read AD 27, 28, 29, 30?, but the point is that at least a decade had elapsed during which it was the Jewish Church that had the authority, blessing and power of God so evidently displayed upon it.

As the inspirer of Scripture, the Holy Spirit takes great care that we understand the events that led to the conversion of Cornelius (Acts 10 and 11), by repeating the circumstances three times! The Jews were *astonished* that Gentiles could even become believers! (Acts 10:45, 11:18). Imagine that *we* Gentiles might actually come into the blessings of salvation and receive the Holy Spirit just as they had.

For me, this clear time period of an exclusively Jewish Church destroyed the argument that Pentecost marked the start of the universal Church and that God had finished with Israel from the birth of the Church onwards. Clearly God had not finished with Israel by the time we reach Acts 10. It was not just this time lapse from Pentecost till Gentiles came to faith that is significant; but also being aware that the concept that Gentiles' becoming believers was at first unthinkable (Acts 11:18).

Let's press on. Stay with me if you can! In Acts 13, the record of Paul's missionary journeys begins, and the historical narrative has a repetition (13:5), 'When they arrived at Salamis, they proclaimed the word of God in the Jewish synagogues'. At Pisidian Antioch (13:14), 'On the Sabbath they entered the synagogue and sat down'. At Iconium (14:1), 'Paul and Barnabas went *as usual* into the Jewish synagogue', and (17:2) '*as his custom was*, Paul went into the synagogue'. In Athens, Luke writes that Paul was greatly distressed to see that the city was full of idols. So he reasoned in the synagogue . . .' (Acts 17:16–17). His heart was for his own people first and to them he first goes. In Acts 18:1 and 4, at 'Corinth . . . every Sabbath he reasoned in the synagogue . . .' and when 'they arrived at

Ephesus . . . he himself went into the synagogue . . .' (18:19). Returning later to Ephesus, 'Paul entered the synagogue and spoke boldly there for three months' (19:8).

Paul travels to Jerusalem where Luke records that 'many thousands of Jews have believed' (Acts 21:20). The Greek is more likely to mean that tens of thousands had come to faith, and James and the elders continue their report to Paul by saying that 'all of them are zealous for the law'. That in itself stirred up a hornets' nest within me! How was it that the gospel of grace in our Lord Jesus Christ should not have freed them from being zealous for the law?! How come the Holy Spirit actually made them *more* zealous for the law than they (probably) had been before? That issue joined an increasing number of questions that this thesis was raising! What *was* clear was that there had been a very significant movement *within* Judaism, for that is how the early Church had seen itself. They were called a 'Nazarene sect' (Acts 24:5), for to these Jewish believers, Jesus of Nazareth was the Messiah. Even Paul, on his return to Jerusalem (in Acts 21:17 and following) demonstrates his observance of the law as prescribed in Numbers 6:13–20.

Acts closes with Paul still reaching Jews (Acts 28:17). Paul had not given up! After a stormy ride to Rome, it only takes him three days to call together the Jewish leaders, still following the Lord's example of going first to 'the lost sheep of the house of Israel' as all the above references show.

However, his scathing attack upon them, where he quoted from the Book of Isaiah 6:9–10, seemed to be saying that here was the *end* as far as Paul was concerned for the Jews:

Go to this people and say, 'You will be ever hearing but never understanding; you will be ever seeing but never perceiving. For this people's heart has become calloused; they hardly hear with their ears, and they have closed their eyes. Otherwise they might see with their eyes, hear with their ears, understand with their hearts and turn, and I would heal them' (Acts 28:26–27).

By the end of Acts it is clear that Israel are not accepting the gospel as a nation, or even as a majority.

Those words write a subliminal, yet indelible, message into one's heart every time one finishes the Book of Acts, just as the stern words which close the Old Testament in Malachi, '. . . or else I will come and strike the land with a curse' (Mal 4:6). The implicit message is quite simply, 'God has finished with the Jews'. I questioned that perhaps after all, the theory on which I was working (namely that God, in Christ, had a priority in ministry 'first for the Jew'), had ultimately run out of road. A letter from Paul to our Church with a closing quote like that and we would all be feeling written off!

But I checked to see the context of what Paul was quoting. He takes only part of the passage in Isaiah 6, surely aware of the full text, for the prophet immediately follows this part of his message through the Holy Spirit, by asking the question, 'For how long, O Lord?' (Isa 6:11). In other words, for how long would this people (Israel) be for ever hearing and never understanding? The Lord's reply is, '*until* . . .' (Isa 6:11). It is the same 'until' that the Lord Jesus Christ says to Jerusalem as he weeps over it, 'You will not see me again *until* you say, "Blessed is he who comes in the name of the Lord"' (Matt 23:39). It came to me that Paul was not eternally writing off his Jewish brothers in the flesh, but rather seeing that this part of Isaiah's prophecy was, for them, true. Had he not made the same statement to the Jews when almost the whole city of Pisidian Antioch turned out to hear Paul and Barnabas (Acts 13:46), and did he not make it his continued strategy to speak to his people first even when, in any particular place, he was rejected? I would be persuaded later, through Paul's letter to the Romans that he never lost sight of the 'until' of the prophet Isaiah's message of condemnation.

There is an interesting footnote in the NIV for Acts 28:28, which points out that some manuscripts have an additional verse (29), 'After he said this, the Jews left, arguing vigorously amongst themselves'. In a sense, that indicated to me the acknowledgement of their continuing existence as a people – and a very realistic picture is presented – they are still arguing to this day about the divinity of the Messiah.

So, for me, the thesis seemed to be holding, that there *was* a priority in Scripture: God revealing himself *first* to Israel, coming in person to *Israel* first and instructing his followers to go *first* to the lost sheep of the house of Israel. He reveals his resurrection and ascension *only* to Jews. The early Church is made up entirely of Jewish believers up to the conversion of Cornelius (with the difficulties I have mentioned in Samaria and with the Ethiopian) and the Holy Spirit comes *only* upon Jews, and on the very day of Pentecost, the Festival of Weeks (or firstfruits of the harvest), who were already the firstfruits of the Church, as prescribed in the Law of Moses (Ex 34:22). Far from its being 'the birth of the Church', the Lord chose to anoint with power the very Jewish people whom he had already called before his death, resurrection and ascension into heaven. Through Peter's preaching a further 3,000 Jews believe and are baptised. From Pentecost, the Apostles too place a priority on going to the Jewish people first. I was persuaded that the early Church were obedient to the example and command given by the Lord. For me, at least, my theory was still intact. God had *not* finished with Israel!

Remember that this search was a personal one. I was in no position to mix with those whom I might have called the buffs in this particular field and, from conversations with Christians in my circle of friends whom I admired and respected, I realised that I was treading on very dangerous ground. For the most part, 'God has finished with Israel' was the usual reply and I was beginning to feel somewhat marginalised. I wondered why others could not see it. Here was a revelation that was bursting to come out. Had I got this completely wrong?

Why had I not seen this theory before?

As Gentile Christians, we tend to start the Bible more than three-quarters of the way through. That is, we are (rightfully) introduced to Jesus and become familiar with the New Testament *first* and, from there, we gradually get to know the Old Testament. It is therefore *from* a New Testament perspective that we view what we are usually taught is the 'Old', whereas Jesus brought us the New Covenant, explaining it *from* the perspective of his Hebrew Scriptures, as 'The Word became flesh' (Jn 1:14).

Secondly, we usually read short passages of the Bible at a time, often starting a section part way through a chapter, as we do frequently with readings in church, daily reading notes, or daily meditations on selections of promises on different themes. We would therefore miss the thesis of this book which requires more of an overview of the whole Bible. So if this priority to the people of Israel is not the topic in that portion of reading, then we are not alerted to it.

Thirdly, unless we sit at the feet of an Old Testament scholar, we are probably brought up on, or introduced to, preaching that tends to use the Old Testament as a fund of illustrations for better understanding the Christian life. In this sense, Israel can be 'likened' to the Church, and passages such as Paul's words to Corinth, referring to Israel's experiences, reinforce this, 'Now these things occurred as examples to keep us from setting our hearts on evil things as they did' (1 Cor 10:6).

Fourthly, if we have been trained theologically, we will almost certainly have heard teaching that suggests that God has 'replaced' Israel by the Church, known as 'replacement theology' or 'secessionism', which, in turn, leads to the concept of 'dominionism'. (Why is it that we always have to think up long words for these sorts of things?). There are certainly passages that may encourage this view and these can colour the way we look at the Hebrew Scriptures.

Finally, in the wisdom of the Church fathers, we have divided our Bibles into 'Old' and 'New', even marketing the New Testament without the Old Testament, whereas *both* together make up the revelation of God. This encourages the conclusion that the Old Testament and therefore the Israel of the Old Testament can be dispensed with, and that God finishes with them in favour of the New Testament and the Church.

But what was it for me that would integrate *both* Testaments?

Chapter 4

A MASTER-PLAN FOR THE COVENANTS

When I first started to work in London I had no idea how to get around except by Underground. I knew tiny parts of the City or West End centred around Underground stations, but I could not connect one part with the next. I certainly could not say that I was a Londoner, even though I lived there and worked there. It was only as I used road transport and connected up the different parts of London that I began to understand the layout of the capital.

The same had been true of the Bible. I knew certain favourite texts, passages and stories, but I could not connect the whole picture. Where were the main arteries of doctrine that held both Testaments together?

By now, I was seeing the covenants in Scripture with new insight. Without grasping the promises made in the covenants I had no handle with which to grasp the prophecies concerning Israel's future. Here was the breakthrough that I had needed.

All the covenants except the covenant God made with Noah and every 'living creature' (Gen 6:18, 9:8–17), were made with Israel: the Abrahamic covenant (Gen 12:2–3; 15:18–21, 17:1–8, 17–19, etc.), the Mosaic covenant (Ex 19:5–8 and other references), the Levitical covenant (Num 25:12–13, Mal 2:4–5, 8), the Davidic covenant (2 Sam 7:16) and the New covenant (Jer 31:27–34).

The adrenaline, that I believed to be the Holy Spirit, encouraged me to look at the covenants with a renewed interest. Was there an 'Old' covenant that was replaced by a 'New' covenant, or had I missed something?

The covenant with Noah

The covenant with Noah was promised before the Flood (see Genesis 6:18) and confirmed after, when God declared, 'I now establish my covenant with you and with your descendants after you . . . Never again will all life be cut off by the waters of a flood; never again will there be a flood to destroy the earth' (Gen 6:18 and 9:8–11). It concerned every living creature on earth. God gave the sign of a rainbow in the sky, 'I have set my rainbow in the clouds, and it will be a sign of the covenant between me and the earth . . . Whenever the rainbow appears in the clouds, I will see it and remember the everlasting covenant' (Gen 9:13–16).

The nature of God's covenants

Let us stop for a moment to consider the nature and characteristics of God's covenants. The master-plan, the covenant with all peoples through Noah, establishes that the five covenants of God have five characteristics. The first is that they are God's sovereign idea in the first place! Secondly, this covenant through Noah was made to all Creation. The third characteristic is that this covenant was clearly unconditional and the fourth, the rainbow, the sign of promise, was not something man could engineer. The final characteristic of this covenant is that it would be everlasting. We still benefit today from the stability of a world that is not deluged by a destruction, as the antediluvian world was, because of God's faithfulness to what he promised.

God has not forgotten his covenant with Noah, as the rainbow still reminds us today. In brief, here was the steadfast, faithful, Sovereign God, revealing himself to mankind, making unilateral promises in totally God-ordained circumstances, with everlasting consequences.

These characteristics are relevant to his covenants with Israel. Remember that I was coming from the assumption that God had finished with Israel because they had broken their part of God's (later) covenant with them. but I was to find that the characteristics of God's covenant preclude that.

The motorway

In considering the different covenants, an illustration came to me as I was driving to work on the M25, London's busy orbital motorway, known by those who use it as the world's largest long stay car park! The journey usually gave me some time to think.

If God's purposes revealed in the covenants could be thought of in such ways, it seemed to me that it might be possible in some respects to compare the progression of God's unfolding revelation of salvation history from Genesis to Revelation rather like a journey along a motorway.

The lanes of this imaginary motorway run right through Scripture. There is a linear plan of God, and things are *leading* somewhere with Jesus, the 'Alpha and the Omega, the First and the Last, the Beginning and the End' (Rev 22:13). In this analogy it is the covenants that act like the major signposts along the motorway.

Just as the motorways have signposts to show the distances to different destinations and numbered emergency telephone boxes that act rather like marker posts, so we use this concept to date certain sections of this Biblical motorway. For instance, the Living Application Bible (Tyndale, 1988) has a linear chart entitled 'Chronology of Bible and world events' that is laid out rather like a motorway, with the known Biblical dates shown on

one side of the motorway and world events on the other. This
chart particularly illustrates that the world has a different
agenda from that of the Bible. On the Bible side of the motorway it records that in 701 BC, 'Jerusalem is besieged by
Sennacherib', whereas below it, on the other side of the motorway, appears the important announcement, 'False teeth
invented in Italy'!

Finally, just as motorways have signs that tell us which
regions we are travelling through or which special attractions
there are to see, so our motorway through the Scriptures could

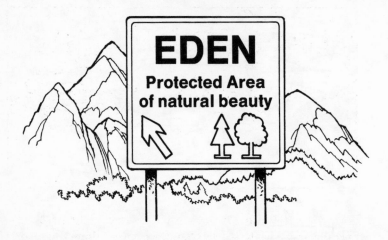

signpost particular distinct events or circumstances of interest as the Biblical account unfolds.

So the motorway illustrates a time sequence of events. But please note: the motorway in this illustration is *not* London's orbital M25, as that would be circular and would merely take us back to the beginning of our journey!

There are five major covenants that concern our theory, and the covenant with Noah provides the master-plan, one that God does not throw away.

Let's travel down the motorway of God's expanding revelation and then see what the covenants (God's signposts) are and where they lead us.

The Abrahamic covenant

Now to the first of the covenants that God made with Israel. To one person, Abram, God reveals his eternal plan of salvation. This plan would involve the promise of a chosen people, a promised land and a special purpose, that is, to be the blessing of all peoples through the Messiah.

Tragically, as soon as man disobeys God's simple command

in the Garden not to eat the fruit of the tree of the knowledge of good and evil, the world attempts to drive along the road of mankind's destiny in the wrong direction.

God has a plan to turn all those around who would be willing to listen and follow him. As with Noah, he wants to save the world. So, from out of all peoples of the world, God chooses to make this promise to Abram, 'I will make you into a great nation'(Gen 12:2)

The great nation, we can term the chosen *People*. God, as it were, creates a contraflow and calls Abram to cross over and travel in the opposite direction and become a great *People*.

Abram, who was descended from Eber and called 'the Hebrew' (Gen 14:13) had to cross over the River Euphrates to get to the land promised to him. This idea of crossing over can be traced back to the root of the word 'Hebrew' which comes from Eber (Gen 10:21), referring to the descendants of Eber meaning 'beyond the river' (*Young's Analytical Concordance*). Joshua (24:2, 3, 14, 15) reminds Israel that their forefathers worshipped 'beyond the River', that is the Euphrates.

God gave to Abram additional promises, 'I will make your name great . . . I will bless those who bless you and whoever curses you I will curse; and all the peoples on earth will be

blessed through you' (Gen 12:2, 3) . . . 'To your offspring I will
give this land' (Gen 12:7).

Let's call the promise 'All peoples on earth will be blessed
through you', the promised *Purpose*. The promise of the land
we might see as the promised *Place*. We note that the promise
would be for ever, God revealing the length of the motorway –
for ever. You could also say 'in *Perpetuity*'.

Over the contraflow lane there might have appeared the following major signpost:-

I promise you a people
I promise you a place
I promise you a purpose
. . . in perpetuity

Here we begin to see the *Plan* of God for the salvation of the
world in these four promises to Abram, whom God renamed,
Abraham (which means 'father of many'): a *People* who would
come from him, a *Place* that they would be given, a *Purpose*
that would bless all peoples and that his promises would be for
ever, or in *Perpetuity*.

We are looking at the motorway analogy, down which the
peoples of the world travel. Warnings and judgments are sign-
posted above the lanes that the world travels along, whereas a
Promise contraflow system is operating through this covenant
with Abraham. We will see that this runs right through into the
New Covenant, and God *amplifies* aspects of the promises as
each covenant unfolds.

The blessing to all peoples

Miles down the motorway, with the benefit of hindsight and
guided by the Holy Spirit, Paul describes the way this *Promise*
contraflow works:

The Scripture foresaw that God would justify the Gentiles by faith, and announced the gospel in advance to Abraham: 'All nations will be blessed through you'. So those who have faith are blessed along with Abraham, the man of faith (Gal 3:8–9).

What he is saying is that through faith in the Messiah, the Gentiles would be blessed and justified and join those in the *Promise* contraflow lane. He thus adds, 'If you belong to Christ, then you are Abraham's seed, and heirs according to the promise' (Gal 3:29).

Israel had to be taught to walk in the promises given to their forefathers. Agreed, not all Israel were in the *Promise* lane, for only those Israelites with faith could travel down this contraflow. They are known as the 'remnant of Israel', and some of these great heroes of faith are listed in the hall of fame in Hebrews 11.

From Abraham, to Isaac and to Jacob

The *Promise* contraflow, repeated frequently in Genesis, passes on from Abraham through to Isaac.

> The Lord appeared to Isaac and said, '. . . For to you and your descendants I will give all these lands and will confirm the oath I swore to your father Abraham . . . and through your offspring all nations on earth will be blessed' (Gen 26:2–4).

God says of the Abraham's eldest son, Ishmael,

> 'I will surely bless him; I will make him fruitful and will greatly increase his numbers. He will be the father of twelve rulers, and I will make him into a great nation. But my covenant I will establish with Isaac' (Gen 17:20–21).

Thus, the firstborn natural son (Ishmael) is set aside in favour of the child born of promise (Isaac).

The line of promise was next made to Jacob at Beersheba, in preference to firstborn Esau (Paul has something to say about this in Romans 9:10–14). Jacob had a dream in which he saw a stairway to heaven, and the angels of God were ascending and descending on it (Gen 28:12).

> There above it stood the Lord, and he said, 'I am the Lord, the God of your father Abraham and the God of Isaac. I will give you and your descendants the land on which you are lying . . . All peoples on earth will be blessed through you and your offspring. I am with you and will watch over you wherever you go, and I will bring you back to this land. I will not leave you until I have done what I have promised you' (Gen 28:13–17).

God renamed Jacob. 'Your name will no longer be Jacob, but Israel, because you have struggled with God and with men and have overcome' (Gen 32:28).

The *Promise* contraflow then travels on, through the twelve families (or tribes) of Israel (Gen 49:1–28).

God is faithful, and Mary, the mother of Jesus, discerned his faithfulness to the covenant he had made nearly 2,000 years earlier with Abraham, when she rejoiced over the Child of Promise in her womb, 'He has helped his servant Israel, remembering to be merciful to Abraham and his descendants for ever, even as he said to our fathers' (Lk 1:54–55). God had *not* forgotten the promises made to Abraham, Isaac and Jacob. They still stood, just as he said they would – for ever.

So our motorway takes us onwards, past the patriarchs and into the book of Exodus.

Chapter 5

A CHOSEN PEOPLE – BUT WHY?

When God made another covenant with Moses, to which we now turn, I questioned whether he had broken his former covenants with Noah and Abraham. But if he had, then the term 'everlasting' has no currency at all. I looked up the word in a concordance and saw just how many references there are concerning God's promises to Israel as being everlasting. It is overwhelming!

I had rather simplistically thought that there was an *Old Covenant* and a *New Covenant* and that, basically, the New had replaced the Old. However, I then saw that the covenant that God made with Abraham still stood! Paul is absolutely categorical about it, 'What I mean is this: the law, introduced 430 years later, *does not set aside* the covenant previously established by God and thus do away with the *promise*' (Gal 3:17).

The Law, given through Moses was *added* to the promises made to Abraham, as Paul goes on to say (Gal 3:19), 'What, then, was the purpose of the law? It was *added* because of transgressions'. To *add* something is not to remove what was first there but to *include* it in addition. Paul concludes, 'Is the law, therefore, opposed to the promises of God? Absolutely not!' (Gal 3:21).

It was in thinking about the promises of a *People*, a *Place*, a

Purpose and the concept of in *Perpetuity* that I was reminded of, strangely, a pack of cards! I now saw that the covenants can be seen to be *progressive*. They assume the previous ones and *unfold* God's purposes step by step, and each one *expands* and develops aspects of the previous ones.

The word to 'make' a covenant comes from the same root as 'cut' (Hebrew, *karath, Young's Analytical Concordance*), hence circumcision as a sign of the covenant and the symbolism acted out in Genesis 15:9–10, 17. To go back to the pack of cards, the dealer asks for the pack to be cut and divided. It is the dealer's initiative to place the cards as he wishes. There are four suits, and I was seeing that these four promises are somewhat like the four suits. As cards from each suit are dealt in order, face up, and successively higher cards are placed on each suit, so with each successive covenant and promise, more is revealed of God's purposes. Eventually, each promise reveals the royal cards and, though there is a joker in the pack (no guesses as to who he might be), God always holds the aces in the end!

It seemed obvious to me that if God were to break one covenant, then why could he not break the rest? As in the illustration of the pack of cards, there would be no foundation on which to build the rest of the pack. The covenant with Moses was added to the covenants already made with Noah and Abraham.

The promised 'chosen' people

In the book of Exodus we find the Children of Israel in slavery in Egypt and the account of how God calls Moses to lead them out of slavery into the Promised Land.

The twelve tribes that came from the twelve sons of Jacob, now renamed 'Israel', become God's chosen people, and Moses tells them,

> 'The Lord did not set his affection on you and choose you because you were more numerous than other peoples, for you were the fewest of all peoples. But it was because the Lord loved you *and kept the oath* he swore to our forefathers . . .' (Dt 7:7).

A study in a concordance on the words 'oath' and 'swore' made me realise just how much God is wanting us to know that he is *on oath* to fulfil all the promises made to the Patriarchs.

What had been a chosen family grew to become a chosen nation. Again I struggled with the whole question of favouritism. Why should God choose *one* group and not another? But Romans 2:11 says that 'God does not show favouritism'. Rather he chooses people *for a Purpose*, and we have seen how he *chose* the line through Isaac and Jacob.

I had always been brought up with the phrase that Israel were the chosen people, but I had little idea *why* they were so called! Now that I was seeing this covenant relationship in a new light, the picture became clearer. I look back and see how central this is to the question, 'Has God finished with Israel?'

He chose Israel for a number of reasons. Firstly, they would record for all time the revelation of God in Scripture for all peoples. God chose the temperament, culture and worldview of the Hebrews to convey to us what he is like. He could have chosen another ethnic group, but he didn't!

I remember seeing a television documentary commemorating the 40 years of Queen Elizabeth II's reign. During the programme the camera showed her having her portrait painted, and in one frame we could see the canvas and artist painting, with liberal quantities of oil paint. Further from the camera, and in the same frame, her Majesty. What struck me was that whilst the emerging portrait was a likeness of the Queen, it would not have been my choice of style. The point that came to me was that this artist was the Queen's choice, not my own. She was happy that he should represent her likeness on canvas even if I was not.

In a similar way, God chose the Israelites to represent his likeness in setting them aside to record the Scriptures. They had no problem with literalism, as the Western mind does. For them there was no division between the secular and the sacred. They could handle the anthropomorphisms, that is the many conceptions and representations of God in Scripture that suppose him as having the form, personality or attributes of a human being. They were able to hold together paradoxes where things appeared in opposition to each other, for instance, God's sovereignty in predestination and man's free choice. They had corporate values that we have exchanged for individualism. Finally, being of Middle Eastern temperament, they understood and could record the extremes of the heat of God's love for them as revealed in Scripture as well as the heat of his wrath. Did not Jesus warn the church at Laodicea, 'You are neither cold nor hot. I wish you were either one or the other! So, because you are lukewarm – neither hot nor cold – I am about to spit you out of my mouth' (Rev 3:15, 16). Consider how striking we find the heat of Jesus' criticisms of the Jewish leadership. But speaking heatedly is typical Middle Eastern temperament and foreign to our Western culture.

It was the Hebrew culture, temperament and worldview that God chose, just as the Queen had chosen that particular artist. If that was his choice and not mine, then who am I to see things differently? If I had a problem with the style that God chose to be the picture that he wanted painted in the Bible, then the problem was my own. I was appreciating my debt to Israel and the Jewish people for the price they paid to bring God's word to me.

Secondly, Israel was chosen to be a light to the Gentiles. '"You are my witnesses", declares the Lord . . . "that I am God"'. (Isa 43:10–12). God's purpose was that the peoples of the world, the Gentiles, would come to hear and believe through the witness of Israel. Perhaps the account of Jonah being sent to Nineveh is the most well-remembered example of the problems of such a call. I have trouble enough sharing my faith with my next door neighbour! Gentiles did find their way into Israel, notably Tamar (Matt 1:3), Rahab (1:5), Ruth (1:5) and Bathsheba (Uriah's wife) (1:6), who were ancestors of the Messiah and prefigured the blessing to all peoples promised to Abraham. They crossed over from the world's lane, into the contraflow lane of *Promise*.

Thirdly, the chosen people of Israel were to be ruled by the Lord of heaven and earth. He called them *his* people ('Let *my* people go', he instructed Moses to tell Pharaoh. See Ex 4:22, 23; 5:1).

Fourthly, they were to *live out* and *demonstrate* a holy relationship of love with him, 'Love the Lord your God with all your heart and with all your soul and with all your strength' (Dt 6:5). They were called to be a *royal priesthood*, 'You will be for me a kingdom of priests and a holy nation' (Ex 19:6).

Fifthly, and as if that were not enough, the Children of Israel were chosen to be an example of God's faithfulness, 'because of the Lord, who is faithful, the Holy One of Israel, who has chosen you' (Isa 49:7).

Finally and supremely, they were to be the people through whom the Messiah would come, 'and from them is traced the human ancestry of Christ, who is God over all, for ever praised!' (Rom 9:5). What an incredible calling to be chosen for such a task. Which of us would voluntarily choose to say 'yes' to all that! What a responsibility it held.

Paul summarises these different aspects of the call upon Israel in Romans 9:4–5 and he uses the *present* tense, 'Theirs *is* the adoption as sons; theirs the divine glory, the covenants, the receiving of the law, the temple worship and the promises. Theirs are the patriarchs and from them is traced the human ancestry of Christ'.

As Golda Meir once said, 'Lord, can't you choose some other people?' What an incredible calling and how quick we are to judge their failings! Sadly, the Exodus from Egypt records all these failings of this representative people as, all but Joshua and Caleb, they disobey the Lord in the wilderness.

It was as though this time they had really discovered London's M25 orbital motorway and travelled round in circles for forty years! God provided service stations at various points along the way, but basically they were lost until God raised a generation in the wilderness who would be led by Moses to the very edge of the Promised Land and by Joshua into the land. The time of judgment had come upon the inhabitants of the land of Canaan (Gen 15:16, Dt 9:5).

So the chosen family who had become the *Promised People* were chosen to live in the Promised Land. From now on, the land (the Promised *Place)* is the setting of most of the rest of the Hebrew Scriptures.

The promised place

God confirms with Moses the promises that he swore to Abraham, Isaac and Jacob some 430 years earlier, when he says:

> 'I am the Lord. I appeared to Abraham, to Isaac and to Jacob as God Almighty . . . I also established my covenant with them to give them the land of Canaan . . . *and I have remembered my covenant* . . . I am the Lord, and I will bring you out from under the yoke of the Egyptians. I will free you from being slaves to them, and I will redeem you with an outstretched arm and with mighty acts of judgment. I will take you as my own people, and, I will be your God. Then you will know that I am the Lord your God, who brought you out from under the yoke of the Egyptians. And I will bring you to the land I swore with uplifted hand to give to Abraham, to Isaac and to Jacob. I will give it to you as a possession' (Ex 6:2–8).

It is interesting that the promises contained in this passage ('I will bring you out . . . I will free you . . . I will redeem you . . . I will take you as my own people') become the structure of the Passover meal, with four cups remembering the four 'I will's' of their redemption and a fifth cup (of Elijah) remembering the promise of the Land. Our Communion service took on a new depth of meaning for me as I learned that the observant Jewish Jesus, soon to be the Lamb of God, who would take away the sins of the whole world, had taken perhaps the third cup, the cup of blessing and redemption at the last supper – 'and I will redeem you with an outstretched arm' – as he inaugurated the New Covenant in his blood. It was to be with arms outstretched on the cross that he would redeem us.

Later, when the Children of Israel sinned in the desert by making an idol in the form of the golden calf, we are told that God's anger burned against Israel, so that he would destroy them. Moses interceded on behalf of the people. He prayed, 'Why should the Egyptians say, "It was with evil intent that he brought them out, to kill them in the mountains and to wipe them off the face of the earth"?' (Ex 32:12). A fair observation! It would seem that Moses was appealing to God's reputation, and for most of us keeping our reputation is sufficient incentive to make us restore a right impression of ourselves. But the Lord does not relent at this approach. It is only as Moses continues:

> 'Remember your servants Abraham, Isaac and Israel *to whom you swore by your own self:* "I will make your descendants as numerous as the stars in the sky and I will give your descendants all this land I promised them, and it will be their inheritance for ever". *Then* the Lord relented' (Ex 32:13–14).

God had bound himself by oath in making all these promises.

Forty years later, Moses instructs the people before they enter the land. He tells them, 'The Lord your God is a merciful God; he will not abandon or destroy you or *forget the covenant* with your forefathers, which he *confirmed* to them by oath' (Dt 4:31).

The covenants illustrate God's faithfulness, and the Exodus from Egypt becomes *the* example of God's faithfulness throughout Scripture, and as I have said before, every year at Passover, this mighty sign of God outworking his covenant promises is remembered.

In the road atlas of Scripture, God had described where they were going. It was a land 'flowing with milk and honey' (Ex 3:8). It was to be a land of 'rest' (Dt 12:9–10) and the land was, from God's perspective, at 'the centre of the nations' (Ezek 5:5 RSV). The 'Mappa Mundi' in Hereford Cathedral is an illustration, and shows Jerusalem and the Holy Land in the centre of the world with the continents of Europe, Asia and (North) Africa around it.

God called it 'my land' (Ezek 36:5), yet also 'your own land' (Ezek 36:24). 'The most beautiful inheritance of any nation' (Jer 3:19) and 'the most beautiful of all lands' (Ezek 20:6). However, Israel needed to be reminded that it always belonged to God for 'the land must not be sold permanently, because the land is mine' (Lev 25:23). He instituted the Jubilee (fiftieth) year when land had to revert to its original clans. It was therefore always a gift from the Lord and never their right to own. It would be a land that would prosper when Israel lived there and would languish when they had to leave through disobedience (Dt 28:38ff). Most relevant of all to their history, occupancy of the land could be taken away (Dt 28:64). Nevertheless the covenant concerning the land remained an everlasting covenant.

My struggle with this whole subject was the question of the land, the circumstances surrounding the formation of the secular state of Israel, and the repeated news broadcast pictures of conflict in the land. I was aware that no side was whiter than white, but this promise in favour of Isaac and not Ishmael raised enormous questions concerning the Arab nations and the constant tensions in the Middle East. How could God favour one people and not another?

I was wrestling with the question, 'Has God finished with Israel?', then came upon a wonderful purpose for the Arab people, which is outside the scope of this book to develop. We have a brief glimpse into that promise in Isaiah, 'In that day Israel will be the third, along with Egypt and Assyria, a blessing on the earth. The Lord Almighty will bless them, saying, "Blessed be Egypt my people, Assyria my handiwork and Israel my inheritance"' (Isa 19:24–25). And, as mentioned in the previous chapter, God said of Ishmael, 'I will surely bless him; I will make him fruitful and will greatly increase his numbers. He will be the father of twelve rulers, and I will make him into a great nation' (Gen 17:20).

There was still work to do over the issue of the land! Why was the New Testament so silent on the question of the land? The promise was to be in *Perpetuity*. That the land rightfully belonged to Israel is not questioned, as the people of Israel were *in* the land promised to them. It was even called the land of Israel (Matt 2:21). Did Jesus' coming make the promise of the land irrelevant? Was it not more accurate to see that in the New Testament the issue that so vexed the Jewish people was the *occupation* of the land by the Romans?

In one way, I could see that there was silence on the issue in the same way as there is silence in Britain as to whether we would benefit were we to have a monarchy. It seemed the argument was the same. We *have* monarchy and the debate would be realistic were we to *lose* the monarchy. They *had* the land (though it was occupied). The debate arises once they lose the land that they were promised.

The promised purpose

To continue, the *Promise* that through Abraham's offspring, all peoples on earth would be blessed still had far greater revelation to follow. It would include nothing less than the presence of the loving God, Creator of heaven and earth, the God of Abraham, Isaac and Jacob, in the Person of Jesus Christ, who came that we should have eternal life (Jn 3:16).

This same loving presence of God appeared to Moses in a burning bush, and then in dramatic form, in the accounts of the Exodus from Egypt, through mighty signs and wonders, the plagues, the Passover, the parting of the Red Sea, the pillar of cloud to guide them during the day and pillar of fire at night. He would appear to them in the Tabernacle, and Moses would meet with him face to face at Mount Sinai.

The *Purpose* strand of God's promise could be summarised in the following command, 'Hear O Israel: The Lord our God, the Lord is one. Love the Lord your God with all your heart . . .' (Dt 6:4–5), reaffirmed by the One who came to be the blessing, when Jesus spelt out this as 'the most important' commandment (Mk 12:29–30).

I got so muddled over God's covenant through Moses (Jewish Rabbis identify 613 commandments) and the legalism that resulted, that I had missed God's central purpose of a loving relationship. But it was through what we refer to as "the law" (the covenant with Moses) that the loving God would reveal himself, his nature and his character. Here was his purpose, to call his people into a loving relationship with him. The Ten Commandments were given because of his love. He precedes the giving of them by speaking of that special relationship which he had with them in the words, 'I am the Lord your God . . . you shall not . . .' I had majored on the 'you shall nots', that is all the laws. He emphasises, 'I am the Lord your God' (Dt 5:6f). I soon discovered that what I had clumsily parcelled up as "law", with all the negative imagery, of rules and regulations, of being caught by "the law", and of legalism, was such a different concept in God's eyes. It was Torah, meaning teaching, direction and instruction.

Paul said that the covenant with Moses was rather like a trustee or guardian appointed to lead us to the Messiah, Jesus Christ (Gal 3:24). How could God do away with the law as long as there are still a people who need to find the Messiah as a result of the law? The law reveals transgressions and shows us the character of the holy, loving God. We see now that the law pointed to Jesus Christ.

It is worth seeing that the law was given to the Children of Israel *before* they entered the Promised Land in order that they became a holy people and the land became the Holy Land. If the analogy of the motorway can be taken even further, the Ten Commandments and all the other laws that God gave following them could be likened to traffic cones that were given to guide *People* within the *Promise* lane of God's *Purpose* and blessing!

I suppose a lot of people must have wished that they had gone into the traffic cone making business. They could have made a fortune! It is as though the Children of Israel went into that business for, instead of being content with God's 613 laws, or traffic cones that were to guide them along his Holy Way of *Promise*, they later introduced thousands of further traffic cones. For example, in place of one of God's commands, 'Remember the Sabbath day by keeping it holy' (Ex 20:8), they were later to create 1,500 more in the form of rabbinical laws to make sure that they did not wander off the contraflow and so break that *one* commandment. In that way, it might be argued that keeping the Sabbath holy became the most onerous day in the week!

So the four elements of God's covenant with Abram back in Genesis 12 still stood: a *People*, a *Place*, a *Purpose*, and all these in *Perpetuity*. But why was their history a picture of such frequent rejection by God?

Chapter 6

BLESSINGS AND CURSES

Within the covenant through Moses, the people had a choice, for Moses had prophesied:

> Be careful not to forget the covenant of the Lord your God . . . After you have had children and grandchildren and have lived in the land a long time – if you then become corrupt and make any kind of idol, doing evil in the eyes of the Lord your God . . . I call heaven and earth as witnesses against you this day that you will quickly perish from the land that you are crossing the Jordan to possess. You will not live there long but will certainly be destroyed. The Lord will scatter you among the peoples . . . (Dt 4:23–27).

Later, the options are spelled out more clearly, that within the covenant, there are blessings and there are curses. The reader would be wise to read Deuteronomy 28:1–14 to see what blessings God would bestow upon an obedient Israel. Imagine what a blessing these verses describe for any nation! Because the blessings of the covenant are conditional upon obedience, so too are the curses of Deuteronomy 28:15 to the end of the chapter resulting from disobedience. (These need to be read as the next paragraphs will be meaningless without so doing.)

I had assumed that all the troubles of Israel and the Jewish people throughout history were a result of a *broken* covenant, but the point here is that disobedience led to the curses *within* the covenant to come into operation. Were God to have abandoned the covenant that he made with Israel through Moses, then we would hardly see the incredible accuracy and enormous sadness of so much of the Jewish people's tragic history as these curses come about! The fact that we have seen Israel scattered on two occasions in their history and persecuted so much is because God has bound himself by oath to his covenant, to the promises of blessing *as well as* to its curses.

So for Israel, it is to be either health or sickness, wealth or poverty, status or disgrace, peace or war. Disobedience does not break God's covenant promises, but brings upon Israel the sanctions contained in the covenant. Was my rejection of the sternness of God the reason why the holy fear and awe of him had largely disappeared from my understanding of his nature and character? Scripture reveals God as God of curses as well as blessings and that was offensive to me.

I realise that this sounds so negative, but struggling with this concept has helped me enormously in explaining how it was that most Jewish people could be in the Diaspora, and even far way from the Messiah, and yet still be *within* the covenanted purposes of God as chosen people.

As we continue down the motorway of salvation history, it is evident that the covenant allowed for Israel's disobedience, for in his mercy, God also allowed for Israel's restoration:

'Yet in spite of this, when they are in the land of their enemies, I will not reject them or abhor them so as to destroy them completely, *breaking my covenant with them*. I am the Lord their God. But for their sake I will remember the covenant with their ancestors . . .' (Lev 26:44–45).

Even God's sanctions contain the promise of restoration.

But is not the Mosaic covenant conditional?

So strong was the confusion that I had over the rejection of the Messiah by Israel and the (apparent) rejection of them by God that this question became an important one for me.

We have seen the everlasting nature of the Abrahamic covenant, yet, in having Ishmael through Hagar, Abraham was also disobedient. However, his disobedience did not cause the covenant to be broken.

The Mosaic covenant brought the children of Israel into the privileged place of becoming the people of God. The conditions of the covenant and the call to obedience merely reveal how they could maintain the continued enjoyment of its privileges and blessings.

If you think about it, we too, as Gentiles, are similarly called to obey the Lord Jesus Christ as we trust and follow him. The same conditions are upon us too.

If we say of the Israelites that they disobeyed the covenant with Moses and it was conditional, then what of us! Jesus said, 'If anyone does not remain in me, he is like a branch that is thrown away and withers; such branches are picked up, thrown into the fire and burned' (Jn 15:6), and Paul speaks of our (Gentile) grafting into the olive tree and failing to stand by faith, 'For *if* God did not spare the natural branches [Israel], he will not spare you either' (Rom 11:21). To the Corinthians, Paul wrote, 'By this gospel you are saved, *if* you hold firmly to the word I preached to you. Otherwise, you have believed in vain' (1 Cor 15:2), and to the Colossians, '*if* you continue in your faith . . .' (Col 1:23).

The writer to the Hebrew believers has the same view, 'And we are his house, *if* we hold on to our courage and the hope of which we boast' (Heb 3:6) for, 'We have come to share in Christ *if* we hold firmly till the end the confidence we had at first' (Heb 3:14), and far more seriously,

'It is impossible for those who have once been enlightened, who have tasted the heavenly gift, who have shared in the Holy Spirit, who have tasted the goodness of the word of God and the powers of the coming age, *if* they fall away, to be brought back to repentance, because to their loss they are crucifying the Son of God all over again and subjecting him to public disgrace' (Heb 6:4–6).

Again, '"But my righteous one will live by faith. And *if* he shrinks back, I will not be pleased with him" [quoting Hab 2:3, 4]. But we are not of those who shrink back and are destroyed, but of those who believe and are saved' (Heb 10:38–39).

Peter writes,

'If they have escaped the corruption of the world . . . and are again entangled in it and overcome, they are worse off at the end than they were at the beginning. It would have been better for them not to have known the way of righteousness' (2 Pet 2:20–21).

Finally, in the messages to the seven churches in the book of Revelation, Jesus Christ makes promises *to those who overcome* (Rev 2:7, 11, 17, 26, 3:5, 12, 21). What if we give up being overcomers?

Because God's word is living and active, then as we read it we will find wonderful promises of salvation for those who obey and warnings for those who disobey. It is not often that we hear it preached that the New Covenant is as conditional as the (so-called) Old. Clearly the New Covenant is as conditional as the Mosaic Covenant, and yet where would I be if my unfaithfulness led God to cease being faithful to his promises in Jesus Christ? As Paul says to Timothy (2 Tim 2:13), 'If we are

faithless, he will remain faithful, *for he cannot disown himself*.'
In spite of two thousand years that had included disobedience
and unfaithfulness, Paul could witness to the amazing track
record of the continued loving faithfulness that God had
showed Israel through his covenants.

Israel (even though the twelve tribes divided and became two
kingdoms) still provided the *Promise* lane that would be the
channel of God's blessing to all peoples. God always kept a
remnant that remained faithful so that Israel was not destroyed.
As Ezra prayed to God, following the return to Judah of some
of the exiles from Babylon,

> 'But now, for a brief moment, the Lord our God has been gracious
> in leaving us a remnant and giving us a firm place in his sanctuary
> . . . What has happened to us [in being exiled] is a result of our evil
> deeds and our great guilt, and yet, our God, you have punished us
> less than our sins have deserved and have given us a remnant like
> this. Shall we again break your commands . . .? Would you not be
> angry enough with us to destroy us, *leaving us no remnant* or survi-
> vor? O Lord, God of Israel, you are righteous! We are left this day
> as a remnant' (Ezra 9:8, 13–15).

It is this remnant that remains in the lane of *Promise* as we shall
see later in Romans.

Chapter 7

FIT FOR A KING

We turn to God's covenant with David, still considering the analogy of the motorway running through Scripture and remembering that the covenants are *progressive*. Each one assumes the previous ones. They *unfold* God's purposes step by step and each one *expands* aspects of the previous ones.

The content of the covenant with David is given through Nathan, the prophet. 'The Lord himself will establish a house for you . . . I will establish the throne of his kingdom for ever . . . Your house and your kingdom shall endure for ever before me; your throne shall be established for ever' (2 Sam 7:11b–16 and cf 1 Chron 17:10b–14 and Ps 89:26–29, 33–35, Jer 33:20, 21, 25, 26).

The lane of *Promise* with the four distinctive parts, the promised *People*, the promised *Place*, the promised *Purpose* and in *Perpetuity*, continues even through Israel's high points and low points. On hearing of God's covenant with him, concerning the promised *People*, the chosen race of Israel, David prayed,

'. . . How great are you, O Sovereign Lord! There is no-one like you, and there is no God but you, as we have heard with our own ears. And who is like your people Israel – the one nation on earth that God went out to redeem as a people for himself . . . and to perform

great and awesome wonders by driving out nations and their gods
from before your people, whom you redeemed from Egypt? *You
have established your people Israel as your very own for ever'* (2 Sam
7:22–24).

David was in no doubt about God's covenant faithfulness. Had
God finished with Israel? Not as far as David was concerned.

The Promised Land

During this period of David's kingship in the Promised Land,
obviously the ownership of the land is not in question. They
have possessed the land and have demanded a king so that they
would be like other nations; indeed God expands the boundar-
ies to almost that of his original promise to Abraham.

Concerning the land, David exclaims,

'He remembers his covenant for ever, the word he commanded, for
a thousand generations, the covenant he made with Abraham, the
oath he swore to Isaac. He confirmed it to Jacob as a decree, to
Israel as an everlasting covenant: To you I will give the land of
Canaan (1 Chron 16:15–18, Ps 105:8–11).

The promised *Purpose* becomes clearer, understanding that
from David will come a king, 'and I will establish the throne of
his kingdom for ever. . .Your house and your kingdom shall
endure for ever before me; your throne shall be established for
ever' (2 Sam 7:13, 16).

In Psalm 89, David confirms his understanding of this
message through the prophet Nathan when he writes of God,
'You said, "I have made a *covenant* with my chosen one, I have
sworn to David my servant, 'I will establish your line for ever'
and make your throne firm through all generations'"' (Ps
89:3–4) and later, in the same Psalm, 'and my covenant with
him will never fail. I will establish his line for ever, his throne as
long as the heavens endure' (vv28, 29).

Crucial to understanding the covenant faithfulness of God, Psalm 89:30–37 declares,

> 'If his sons forsake my law . . . *I will not violate my covenant* or alter what my lips have uttered. Once for all, I have sworn by my holiness – and I will not lie to David – that his line will continue for ever . . .'

We see later how Jesus, Son of David, fulfils these promises.

Speaking of this promised *Purpose*, the psalmists write of this coming King,

> '"I have installed my King on Zion, my holy hill." I will proclaim the decree of the Lord: He said to me, "You are my Son; today I have become your Father. Ask of me and I will make the nations

your inheritance, the ends of the earth your possession. *You will rule them with an iron sceptre . . .*"(Ps 2:6–9).

'Your throne, O God, will last for ever and ever; a sceptre of justice will be the sceptre of your kingdom' (Psalm 45:6. Hebrews 1:8 tells us that this speaks of Jesus).

We have already seen that similar prophecies are read tradition- ally at Christmas: Micah's words (5:2), 'But you, Bethlehem Ephrathah, though you are small among the clans of Judah, out of you will come for me *one who will be ruler over Israel,* whose origins are from of old, from ancient times.'

The New Testament opens with this title, 'A record of the genealogy of Jesus Christ, the son of David' (Matt 1:1). Concerning Jesus fulfilling the promise of being son of David, there can be little dispute; the title is given to him fifteen times in the gospels.

Of Jesus, the angel Gabriel announced to Mary, 'The Lord God will give him the throne of his father David, and he will reign over the house of Jacob for ever; his kingdom will never end' (Lk 1:32–33). Though 400 years had passed, God had not forgotten what he had promised. We considered his kingship in Chapter 2.

In the context of his Second Coming, Jesus says to John, 'I am the Root and the Offspring of David' (Rev 22:16).

The promised perpetuity

The Davidic covenant speaks of *an everlasting kingdom.* The last words of David record his saying, 'Has he not made with me an everlasting covenant, arranged and secured in every part?' (2 Sam 23:5). So secure was this covenant, that God was able to say through Jeremiah,

'If you can break my covenant with the day and my covenant with the night, so that day and night no longer come at their appointed time, then my covenant with David my servant . . . can be broken and David will no longer have a descendant to reign on his throne' (Jer 33:20–21).

Imagine that! God links his faithfulness, expressed in his covenant with David, to the created order of day and night. We live our whole lives trusting in the orderliness of day and night. As day succeeds night and night succeeds day, so we have each day a reminder of God's faithful promise to David that a King would arise from his descendants and rule for ever! In the same way, as we have seen, every time we see a rainbow in the sky, we are reminded that God promises *never* to destroy the earth again through flood.

What kind of kingdom would David have understood by these promises, I wondered, a literal one or a spiritual one? The answer became obvious; he would have taken this to mean that his literal, physical, kingly line would last for ever through his offspring and that, literally, his dynasty would never end! Did God ultimately intend this to be so? My counter arguments were weakening, although I had to keep contending with so many questions, not least the issue of David's literal throne remaining unoccupied. That debate is wider than the subject of this book!

Paul appears to be in no doubt about the future physical rule and reign of Jesus. He first states that Jesus came 'to *confirm* the promises made to the patriarchs', as he writes in Romans 15:8, and then, four verses later, as the climax to his letter to the Romans, he exclaims, 'The root of Jesse will spring up, one who will arise to rule over the nations; the Gentiles will hope in him' (Rom 15:12, referring to Isaiah 11:10).

Why was I not convinced by what, at face value, Paul seemed to be saying? What a glorious hope, yet I felt more confused than hopeful. I was, however, filled with a great desire to study Romans again to see how he came to make this statement.

There is still one further covenant that we need to consider, the one through which I, as a Gentile, had come to faith – the New Covenant.

The new covenant promised first to Israel

Remember that we are testing the thesis that God has a priority to reach his people to whom he is covenanted and that the covenants are *progressive*. Each covenant assumes the previous ones, and each *unfolds* God's purposes step by step, and *expands* aspects of the previous ones and does not nullify them.

I had once thought that Jesus came to unveil the New Covenant in what we call the New Testament and that it was entirely 'Christian'. I had thought that Jewish people could accept their part of the book, but that this New Covenant was the Christian part. As with so much before, I now saw that the New Covenant was made *first* with the people of Israel, with both the house of Israel and the house of Judah, and it appears *first* in the Hebrew Scriptures.

Jeremiah writes,

'"The time is coming," declares the Lord, "when I will make a *new covenant with the house of Israel and with the house of Judah.* It will not be like the covenant I made with their forefathers when I took them by the hand to lead them out of Egypt, because they broke my covenant, though I was a husband to them," declares the Lord. "This is the covenant I will make with the house of Israel after that time," declares the Lord. "I will put my law in their minds and write it on their hearts. I will be their God and they will be my people. No longer will a man teach his neighbour, or a man his brother, saying, 'Know the Lord', because they will all know me, from the least of them to the greatest," declares the Lord. "For I will forgive their wickedness and will remember their sins no more."' (Jer 31:31–34).

The problem was not God's covenant made through Moses, but with Israel who were unable to keep the covenant (both the house of Israel who were exiled to Assyria in 722 BC, to be scattered to the ends of the earth and the house of Judah from whom the Jewish people are descended). So God adds this new covenant. The letter to the Hebrews comments on this, 'But God found fault with the people [Israel]' (Heb 8:8) and then quotes Jeremiah 31:31–34. Because he found fault with the people, he introduces a 'superior' covenant founded on 'better promises' (Heb 8:6). How grateful we are!

I was thrown by this passage for years. I had taken this to mean that the New (Testament) Covenant had literally replaced the Old (Testament) Covenant and therefore all that had been promised before. But the first covenant referred to here is not the Abrahamic covenant but the Mosaic covenant, as chapter 9 verse 1 describes, 'Now the first covenant had regulations for worship and also an earthly sanctuary'. The Abrahamic covenant had nothing to do with regulations for worship or a tabernacle. So God was finding fault, not with the Abrahamic covenant, but with the Mosaic covenant in that the law had become *externalised* and Israel had failed to keep it. Despite this, in their worst moments of apostasy to God's loving purpose, with exile to Babylon the only (and imminent) remedy for their sins, he adds, 'I will be their God . . .' (Jer 31:33).

This New Covenant was altogether superior to the covenant with Moses in that he promised, 'I will put my laws in their minds and write them on their hearts' (Heb 8:10, cf Jer 31:33).

I found it helpful to discover that in Hebrew, the word 'new' and 'renew' are the same (chadash). The promise of a *new* covenant does not refer to new, in the sense of something that is totally original, in the same way as the new moon is not really new, but a new cycle of the old. Similarly, just as I am a new creation in God's sight (2 Cor 5:17), it is still the 'same old me' that is 'new'!

The New Covenant is, in that sense, a New (or renewed) 'Old Covenant'. So the New Covenant takes the aspect of the Old Covenant concerning the Law in the Mosaic Covenant that had failed (though it was the people that failed, not the covenant).

It is still with the same people Israel, and still has the central command of the Mosaic Covenant, confirmed by Jesus: 'Love the Lord your God with all your heart . . .' (Matt 22:37–40).

Jesus reveals this new covenant first to Israel

Jesus of Nazareth, God's Son, came *first* to Israel and it was at a Jewish meal, the Passover, and in a Jewish home that he inaugurated the New Covenant at what we call the Last Supper.

It was on the cross that he was sacrificed as 'the Lamb of God who takes away the sin of the world' (Jn 1:29), a difficult concept to understand unless one appreciates the 'shadow' or 'type' of the coming Messiah in the Passover lamb that was sacrificed before the Exodus from Egypt or the sacrificial system of the Tabernacle and Temple. Why was it that I had never seen that the lambs had to be 'year-old males without defect' (Ex 12:5)? Yes, Jesus would be without defect, but male lambs are more accurately called rams and year old male rams are at their prime of life, as one sheep farmer told me, the equivalent of a thirty year old man. Even the substitutionary ram caught in the thicket and sacrificed by Abraham instead of Isaac speaks of Jesus. How powerful the picture of the ram is in comparison with my earlier images of a cuddly and helpless lamb but a few days old.

At last the promised *Purpose* has become clear. God, the God of Abraham, Isaac and Jacob, came in the person of Jesus of Nazareth. The 'I am who I am' (Ex 3:14) revealed himself as the 'I am' in Jesus, the light of the world (Jn 8:12), the one who 'before Abraham was born, I am' (Jn 8:58), the good shepherd (Jn 10:14), the resurrection and the life (Jn 11:25), the way and the truth and the life (Jn 14:6). He revealed the way to receive a new heart through his blood shed on the cross and, by faith in him, the free gift of eternal life, first for Jewish people and then for Gentiles.

In bringing the New Covenant to Israel first, with the emphasis of Jesus that he came 'only to the lost sheep of Israel' (Matt 15:24), he does not abolish the law, rather he comes to fulfil the law (Matt 5:17). By the sending of the Holy Spirit he puts his law within our hearts (Eze 36:26–27).

Jesus affirmed the law in the Sermon on the Mount and summarises all the law and the prophets in just two commandments, confirming his loving relationship, '"Hear, O Israel, the Lord our God the Lord is one. Love the Lord your God with all your heart and with all your soul and with all your mind and with all your strength." The second is this, "Love your neighbour as yourself"' (Mk 12:29–31).

What I had not seen was that Jesus was also confirming all the promises made in the Abrahamic covenant,

> 'For I tell you that Christ has become a servant of the Jews on behalf of God's truth, *to confirm the promises made to the patriarchs*' (Rom 15:8), '*theirs* is . . . the Covenants . . . and the promises' (Rom 9:4) . . . 'for God's gifts and his call are irrevocable' (Rom 11:29).

From my search so far explored in chapters 1 to 5, I was seeing that the *Plan* of God declared to Abraham back in Genesis 12 involved a *People*, a *Place,* a *Purpose* given *in Perpetuity* and ran right through to the end of the Acts of the Apostles. At what point in time did God ever cease to be the God of Abraham, Isaac and Jacob?

Had God finished with Israel? I had seen in the covenant with Noah that covenants are not contracts. They involve the promise of God, 'Know therefore that the Lord your God is God; he is the faithful God, keeping his covenant of love to a thousand generations of those who love him' (Dt 7:9). They involved his confirmation,

> 'Because God wanted to make the unchanging nature of his purpose very clear to the heirs of what was promised, he confirmed it with an oath. God did this so that, by two unchangeable things in

which it is impossible for God to lie . . . we have this hope as an anchor for the soul, firm and secure' (Heb 6:17–19).

Finally, they involve his provision of a sacrifice, 'This is why even the first covenant was not put into effect without blood' (see Heb 9:16–28, Matt 26:27–28).

Could God break his covenant?

That is not the nature of the covenants. They are not contracts with terms and conditions that can be broken by God. He makes the *promise*, he makes the *oath*, he provides the *sacrifice*. As with the pack of cards, where the value of the cards increases up to the royal cards, each covenant builds on the previous ones.

What I had called a motorway, God has called a highway. As Isaiah prophesied, 'And a highway will be there; it will be called the Way of Holiness. The unclean will not journey on it; it will be for those who walk in that Way' (Isa 35:8). Jesus is the one whom we follow on that highway of promise; 'I am the way and the truth and the life. No-one comes to the Father except through me' (Jn 14:6).

Along this highway, the promises made ·in the covenants stand as signposts, the promised *People*, the promised *Place*, the promised *Purpose* and in *Perpetuity*. All of us must cross over from the way of the world onto this Holy way. It would be a highway that John the Baptist would announce (Isa 40:3, Matt 3:3)

There were still too many nagging doubts. I still had to work through the letter to the Romans to see whether the Apostle Paul held that God had yet to finish with Israel. Too many counter arguments bombarded me. Would this question ever find a satisfactory answer?

Chapter 8

THE LETTER TO THE ROMANS

This was where my theory, that God has *not* finished with Israel, would hang or fall. I had to be persuaded that Paul, as the apostle to the Gentiles, could also guide me to see what place Israel still had in God's purposes. Paul's letter to the Romans had to hold the key as his chapters 9, 10 and 11 were so obviously supporting the theory: 'Did God reject his people? By no means!' (Rom 11:1). I had been told that these chapters were a parenthesis or were unrelated to the rest of the letter. Indeed, I have even spoken to one New Testament theologian who said that these chapters mean the very opposite of what the text says! There were still so many questions to ask. Certainly I was nowhere near ready to understand what was meant by 'all Israel will be saved' (11:26) or how to find a way of interpreting it.

There was a problem in the church at Rome, and Paul needed to write to them about it. Luke records in Acts 18 that 'Claudius [the Roman emperor] had ordered all the Jews to leave Rome' (Acts 18:2) This was in AD 49 or 50 (F.F. Bruce, *Acts of the Apostles*, Marshall: 1977). A few years later, Nero allowed them to return to Rome, and this seemed to have caused strains in their relationships as they rejoined their Gentile brothers in the Lord.

For the returning Jews who believed in Jesus as the Messiah, there was an adjustment to make – the church was now run by Gentiles! The letter of Paul indicates that Gentiles were judgmental of the believing Jews because they were still wrestling with the law, issues which looked perilously close to justification by works, whereas Gentiles did not come to faith from a background of the law. Thus we see the issues of righteousness by faith and the example of Abraham addressed in Paul's letter to the church in Rome. The believing Jews were judgmental towards the Gentiles because they were not descended from Abraham in the flesh. Equally, the Gentiles had a problem in that they needed to know God's future purposes for the Jews. All this created tensions which Paul needed to write to them about, together with not a little admonishment about judging one another and the need for acceptance and love.

As I studied this letter, I began to see the line of argument that had previously escaped me. The place of the Jewish person and Israel in God's purposes ran right through the whole letter! Paul was qualified to write to both Jews and Gentiles. Once the Pharisee of Pharisees (Acts 23:6, Phil 3:5), and now both the apostle to the Gentiles (Gal 2:7), and the one who was 'to carry my [Jesus'] name . . . before the people of Israel' (Acts 9:15).

So he challenges both groups within the church, 'let us have peace through our Lord Jesus Christ' (Rom 5:1b NIV footnote), 'let us stop passing judgment on one another (14:13), 'Let us therefore make every effort to do what leads to peace . . .' (14:19), 'Accept one another' (15:7).

Let's look at Paul's line of argument. Remember my quest. I was trying to integrate the teaching of chapters 9 –11 so that I could be satisfied that I was reading them correctly and not lifting them out of context.

I was all right with Chapter 1, as I had no problem accepting the universality of sin and because verse 16 contained the concept that I was exploring, 'I am not ashamed of the gospel, because it is the power of God for the salvation of everyone who believes: *first* for the Jew, *then* for the Gentile'. The same priority is repeated in Chapter 2 verse 9 and also verse 10, the Jews are *first* when it comes to 'trouble and distress' and *first* when it comes to 'glory, honour and peace'. I believed that my theory was holding.

Chapter 2:17 gave me a clue to the way Paul was laying out his line of thought, 'Now you, if you call yourself a Jew . . .'. Paul was speaking to Jews. Indeed, I believe that he started speaking to the Jews back in verse 1, where it reads, 'You, therefore, have no excuse, you who pass judgment on someone else [ie the Gentiles, because they were not descended in the flesh from Abraham] . . .' It makes sense that he is speaking to Jews because in verses 14 and 15, he speaks of Gentiles as 'they'.

I hit a crisis almost immediately! By the time Paul gets to verse 28, he kills my theory stone dead. 'A man is not a Jew if he is only one outwardly, nor is circumcision merely outward and physical'. So it was true after all, I thought! The Jews are no more than a race like any other race now that the New Covenant has come.

Well, in one sense it was a relief. I was becoming a little disturbed that I was getting obsessed with this subject. I had often prayed that if this were not of God, then he would take this theory away and I could get on with living out a normal Christian life. Yet every day, this particular priority in Scripture shouted at me. So I left this problem verse (Rom 2:28) and kept going.

This became another 'Yes, but . . .!' passage, and some of my thoughts on these are in Chapter 12.

The model railway

I was wrestling with piecing together the sections of Paul's letter to the Romans leading up to Chapters 9–11 when, one day, I was visiting a retired Anglican clergyman who had a model railway which was truly magnificent. (Why so many Anglican clergy like model railways, I am not sure, and it is outside the scope of this book to find out!). He could run three trains simultaneously on different sections of the layout. But what struck me was the trackwork. It was superbly laid out section by section, track by track, and it was through this that God spoke to me.

It was as though the trackwork of the model railway had an application to the letter to the Romans. I saw that the letter is laid out, section by section, argument by argument, and, like the track, a particular line of argument runs right through it. I had only ever seen Romans as a series of somewhat disconnected sections, but now the layout of the letter became clear.

The sections of the model railway track were joined together with little metal clips called fishplates. Each section of track clipped into two fishplates, thereby joining them and enabling the power to be transmitted through each section of track. Disconnect the track from the fishplates and the power would cease to flow through each section of track. That had happened for me with Paul's letter to the believers in Rome. By dismantling the different sections of the letter in the past, I had prevented the power of Paul's argument (and thus the witness of the Holy Spirit) from running right through the whole letter. Little wonder Chapters 9–11 had lost their meaning. They had become disconnected.

When I had got to Chapter 2, verse 28, I had become stuck. I could not work out why. Then I saw that Chapter 3 started back on the subject of the Jews. Seeing the model railway layout, however, had also reminded me that on any track there could be some fairly tight bends. I knew that, because when I was a small boy, I had had a model railway and found it great fun to drive the train as fast as I could at the sharpest bend and watch it come off the track. Now I realised that I had come off the track at 2:28. 'A man is not a Jew if he is only one outwardly,

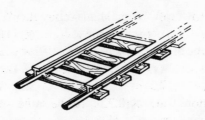

nor is circumcision merely outward and physical.' The unbelieving Jewish people appeared to be written off completely.

Had I not taken the hairpin bend in the track at 2:28 so fast, I would have stayed on the track to find that the direction of Paul's reasoning turns back on itself in 3:1 and continues on with the same thrust of argument, by addressing the issue of the place of the Jews in God's purposes.

'What advantage, then, is there in being a Jew, or what value is there in circumcision? *Much in every way!*' (Rom 3:1, 2). So Paul had not been writing off Jews at all. There is a play on words here, as the word 'Jew' is derived from Judah (Rom 2:29b) which means 'praise' (Gen 29:35 and NIV footnote). The term 'Jew' appears around 191 times and is never used to describe a Gentile. Far from widening the word 'Jew' so that you or I could call ourselves Jews, Paul is if anything, narrowing his definition of a 'true Jew' to those Jews who are a praise to God (2:29). In a similar way, Jesus called Nathanael 'a true Israelite' (Jn 1:47) and that was indeed praise from God!

You may think this all sounds rather academic, but I have heard eminent Christians call themselves the true Jews.

I then saw the 'fishplates'. They were the link words that connected the different sections of Paul's letter. 'What advantage then . . .' (3:1), 'What if . . .' (3:3), 'But if. . .' (3:5), 'What shall we conclude then?' (3:9), 'Now we know . . .' (3:19), 'But now . . .' (3:21), 'Where then . . .?' (3:27) and on into Chapter 4. 'What then shall we say. . .?' (4:1), 'Is this. . .' (4:9), 'Therefore . . .' (4:16), 'Therefore . . .' (5:1), 'You see . . .' (5:6), 'Therefore . . .' (5:12), 'But . . .' (5:15), 'Consequently. . .' (5:18) (Paul cannot seem to stop!), 'What shall we say then?' (6:1), 'If . . .' (6:5), 'Now . . .' (6:8), 'In the same way . . .' (6:11), 'What then? . . .' (6:15), 'Do you not know . . .?' (7:1), 'What shall we say . . .?' (7:7), 'Did that . . .?' (7:13), 'We know . . .' (7:14), 'So I find . . .' (7:21), 'So then. . .' (7:25b), 'Therefore . . .' (8:1), 'Therefore . . .' (8:12), 'We know that. . .' (8:22), 'In the same way . . .' (8:26), 'What, then, shall we say . . .?' (8:31).

The fishplates (and you need lots of them to build a worthwhile track) had led me, in one sequential theme to Romans 9–11. The theme of God's purpose for the Jewish people, far from being a people whom he has written off, becomes the main substance of the letter.

I had heard Chapters 9–11 expounded in isolation from the rest of the letter. Imagine my joy to find that they were central to the whole letter. We will look at this in a moment.

I sped through Chapters 9–11. The little fishplates did not stop even there. The little connectors that were so vital to keep the flow of current running through the track, were still employed by Paul . 'Therefore . . .' (12:1), 'For . . .' (12:3), and then Paul goes into the heart of the second half of his letter concerning how to behave as Jewish and Gentile believers.

In Chapter 12 I had always struggled with the quotation in verse 20. It comes from Proverbs 25 (verses 21, 22). In verse 9 he says, 'Love must be sincere' and then tells us how our love can be sincere by saying, 'If your enemy is hungry, feed him; if he is thirsty, give him something to drink. In doing this, you will heap burning coals on his head.'

To my Gentile, Western way of thinking, I could not see how heaping burning coals on someone's head could be very loving! In fact it seemed the opposite, for my sinful nature could easily feel like doing that to an enemy.

By now I was beginning to dip into books where a Hebraic understanding was opening up Scriptures in a way that the Greek had not been doing, and I found an answer to this problem verse. The writer was Jewish and so was the culture. In the Middle Eastern culture of the day, hospitality was the bottom line as far as social custom was concerned. Thus, if your enemy were hungry, you would give him or her something to eat, and if he or she were thirsty, you would give them something to drink. What was meant by the words, 'In doing this, you will heap burning coals on his head,' was that, if his fire were to go out he could not cook his food, no matter how hungry he was, nor could he warm himself, nor have any source of light. By allowing him to bring round his brazier, which he would carry *on his head*, as was the custom, you would express your love in action by heaping burning coals from your fire onto his head and send him on his way rejoicing! A much more wholesome example of love in action.

That was a digression. Onwards, then, through Chapter 12. Paul continues with these link words: 'Everyone . . .' (13:1), drawing together both Jews and Gentiles. 'Therefore. . .' (14:13), 'Let us therefore . . .' (14:19), 'So whatever . . .' (14:22), 'Accept one another . . .'(15:7).

Paul had kept a consistent argument running through his letter, from the issue in Rome of judgment within the church to his summary to the Gentiles, as to why it was so important that they worked at their relationship with the Jewish believers, 'For I tell you that Christ has become a servant of the Jews on behalf of God's truth, to *confirm* the promises made to the patriarchs so that the Gentiles may glorify God for his mercy' (15:8–9).

As a vicar I had prepared many people for confirmation. To confirm means 'to strengthen, to fix or establish, to ratify, to verify, to assure' (*Chambers*). Paul had, right from Chapter 3 been confirming why the Jews 'have much advantage in every way' (3:1).

In confirming the covenants with Abraham, Isaac and Jacob, as well as the covenant made with David (he too is described as a patriarch by Peter in Acts 2:29), the Lord Jesus presumably confirmed the four elements of the covenants, the promised *People*, the promised *Place*, the promised *Purpose* and all these being in *Perpetuity*, for I was still unable to discover where it is supposed he discards the Abrahamic covenant. As well as 'so that the Gentiles may glorify God for his mercy' (15:9), Paul also says (quoting from different Hebrew Scriptures), 'Rejoice, O Gentiles, with his people [meaning Israel]' (v 10), and again 'Praise the Lord, all you Gentiles, and sing praises to him, all you peoples' (v 11). If Paul had written off Israel, how could he then argue that the Gentiles would glorify God because of what he would do through Israel?

The Bible as a whole was now resonating with an integrity that I had never known before. In seeking to link Scriptures quoted in the New Testament by going back to the Hebrew Scriptures to discover their original context, it became clear that with these quotations in Romans 15:9–12, Paul was coming to the climax of his message, 'The root of Jesse will spring up, one who will arise to rule over the nations; the Gentiles will hope in him' (v 12). What a glorious hope! A veil had been over my eyes all this time.

Paul's prayer in the very next verse was totally appropriate, 'May the God of hope fill you with all joy and peace as you trust in him, so that you may overflow with hope by the power of the Holy Spirit.' He had just spelt out the hope.

ROMANS CHAPTERS 9–11

So to Romans 9–11. The NIV headings immediately become interesting!

1. Chapter 9:1–29   *'GOD'S SOVEREIGN CHOICE'*
2. Chapter 9:30 – 10:21   *'ISRAEL'S UNBELIEF'*
3. Chapter 11:1–10   *'THE REMNANT OF ISRAEL'*
4. Chapter 11:11–24   *'INGRAFTED BRANCHES'*
5. Chapter 11:25–32   *'ALL ISRAEL WILL BE SAVED'*

In chapter 9, Paul is saying that Israel is God's sovereign choice through which he will demonstrate his faithfulness.

From the outset, Paul is talking about Israel and not the church (9:3–5). This could be likened to another of the hairpin bends in the trackwork of Paul's layout. If we come to this section thinking that the church is Israel, we could quite simply leave the track at this point. Martin Luther stopped his commentary on Romans at Chapter 8, probably for this very reason. Paul could hardly be praying for his 'brothers', meaning his 'brothers in Christ', that is members of the church. Why should he wish himself 'cursed and cut off from Christ' (9:3) for those who had come to believe in Jesus as Lord and Messiah? No, he is agonising over the unsaved Jewish people, his brothers in the flesh, 'those of my own race'. How many of us could say that about those unsaved in our family or nation? He repeats his concern, 'my heart's desire and prayer to God for the Israelites is that they may be saved' (10:1). Does the "Church" need saving? (Well, one might argue that some churches do!).

I remember once, when I had only been a Christian for two years, I was helping the chaplain at Wengen in Switzerland. One evening, in the hotel, I found myself sharing with a Jewish student about Jesus. The fact that he was Jewish meant no more to me than if he had been South American or Japanese. I did not see him as religious, indeed he told me quite clearly that he was an atheist and a scientist. Then, quite suddenly, he broke off our conversation because he wanted to watch the current moon landing on television, so we both went to the hotel lounge where the broadcast was under way. We arrived just at the point where Buzz Aldrin, the American astronaut, was reading from Genesis chapter 1, 'In the beginning God created the heavens and the earth . . .' I distinctly felt my Jewish friend's discomfort at an astronaut and scientist reading from the Bible! That, however, is not the point of the story, though it did make me feel rather good at the time. That night, I simply could not sleep, for such was the tremendous burden to pray for that young man. It was not as though I could even claim the concern for him to be my own, I was simply amazed at how much God wanted that man to come to know Jesus the Messiah. Perhaps the Lord was showing me how Paul might have felt, when he said, 'my heart's desire and prayer to God for the Israelites is that they may be saved' (10:1).

In order to see Biblical prophecy clearly, I needed to see first what *already belonged* to Israel, even as the foundations of a building indicate the shape of the building to come. Even though Israel, as a corporate people, was not saved, Paul lists what *is already theirs* because of God's covenant promises as seen in Chapter 4 of this book: 'Theirs *is* the adoption as sons;

theirs the divine glory, the covenants, the receiving of the law, the temple worship and the promises. Theirs are the patriarchs, and from them is traced the human ancestry of Christ' (9:3–5).

If God had written off Israel, Paul would have written, 'Theirs *was* . . .' But he does not, categorically stating 'I ask then: Did God reject his people? *By no means!*' (11:1). That is the strongest negation in the Greek language. Yes, the Jewish people had a problem, 'they did not know the righteousness that comes from God and sought to establish their own' (10:3). They did this by basing their righteousness on works of the law.

From the outset of the letter, Paul has declared that 'in the gospel a righteousness from God is revealed, a righteousness [a "being-made-right-with-God-ness"] that is by faith from first to last' (Rom 1:17) and 'a righteousness from God, apart from the law . . . This righteousness from God comes through faith in Jesus Christ to all who believe [Jew or Gentile]. There is no difference' (3:21–22).

But had God rejected Israel? 'By no means!' (11:1). 'Did they stumble so as to fall beyond recovery? Not at all!' (11:11).

Another hairpin bend had appeared in the track of Paul's argument in 9:6, 'For not all who are descended from Israel are Israel'. I came off the track again!

The principle that I found helpful was to be consistent in the way I approached a verse, just like the driver of a racing car has to take the correct line and speed into a corner in order to find the right line out of it.

Sadly, of this verse, we could also say, 'For not all who are in the church are the church.' Paul is not writing off Israel, but he is saying that some individual Israelites are like the man described in 2:28, 'A man is not a Jew if he is only one outwardly.' He is to say later that these Jewish people are like branches broken off from a natural olive tree (11:17). 'It is the children of the promise who are regarded as Abraham's offspring' (9:8). In other words, to be truly Jewish each has to cross over individually into the *Promise* contraflow lane. They cannot claim physical descent from Abraham as sufficient.

The problem of the word 'law'

Another conflict I was having was with the word 'law'. The word seemed to have the same effect on me as a restricted current has on a model railway engine, first the judder, then the fits and starts and finally a full stop. To borrow our Railway Company's answer to similar problems, there were leaves on the line!

For example, there is a verse in Chapter 7 where Paul laments, speaking to fellow Jews (7:1),

> 'So I find this law at work: When I want to do good, evil is right there with me. For in my inner being I delight in God's law; but I see another law at work in the members of my body, waging war against the law of my mind and making me a prisoner of the law of sin . . .' (7:21–23).

The confusion was the different uses of the word 'law', used on five occasions in this one verse.

The *New Bible Dictionary* (IVP: 1967), points out that there is 'much flexibility in the use of the term "law" (*nomos* in Greek)', and then cites six different ways in which the word is used in the New Testament. The *Jewish New Testament* (David H. Stern, Jewish New Testament Publications: 1989), illustrates this by translating these verses,

> 'So I find it to be the rule, a kind of perverse '*torah*', that although I want to do what is good, evil is right there with me! For in my inner self I completely agree with God's *Torah*, but in my various parts, I see a different '*torah*', one that battles with the *Torah* of my mind and makes me a prisoner of sin's '*torah*', which is operating in my various parts'.

Paul is saying that God's law, the law of Moses, or Torah, is better translated 'teaching, guidance, direction, instruction'. He describes the law as 'holy, righteous and good' (7:12), as 'spiritual' (7:14), and to be upheld (3:31), and he *delighted* in the law (7:22). What visions we have of tortuous rules and regulations. Do I delight that there are thirty mile an hour restrictions on certain open stretches of urban roads? But that's the *law*, employing the same word as Scripture uses for 'teaching'. Paul must have found Psalm 1 a delight.

> Blessed is the man who does not walk in the counsel of the wicked or stand in the way of sinners or sit in the seat of mockers. But his delight is in the law of the Lord, and on his law he meditates day and night (Ps 1:1–2).

Would he not have agreed with David,

> The law of the Lord is perfect, reviving the soul. The statutes of the Lord are trustworthy, making wise the simple . . . They are more precious than gold, than much pure gold . . . By them is your servant warned; in keeping them there is great reward' (Ps 19:7–11)?

How come of all the Psalms, the longest by far is Psalm 119, devoted *entirely* to extolling the law?

It is not the law, in the sense of the teaching, or the word of God in the Torah, that Paul and the author of the letter to the Hebrews are writing off, for that would be to dismiss the very words of God. What is challenged is the twisted (or perverse) 'law' that suggests that law-keeping can enable a person to be righteous in God's sight.

We return, therefore, to Romans 10:4, 'Christ is the *end* of the law.' Another wobbly! Did this mean that God had written off the law? Had his covenant through Moses been annulled and with it his covenant faithfulness? Another crisis of confidence overcame me. If the theory was correct that God had *not* given up on his chosen people nor his covenant with Moses, then I needed to find an alternative interpretation that would demonstrate that God had not written off the law. So I searched through the different translations and found that, although the Authorised Version gives room to allow that God had not demolished the law, 'For Christ is the end of the law for righteousness to everyone that believes', I found no support for my theory from the others.

I still believed that this verse could be read a different way. The Greek word used for 'end' is '*telos*'. We have such an abrupt interpretation of 'end'. For us with a Western mindset, it is more that something has been terminated or dissolved. It describes the termination of something, just as the buffers at the end of a railway track. The Hebrew thinking behind the word 'end' is more like the 'end of one thing that leads to the beginning of another'. For instance, the Hebrew word for summer (*qayits*) shares the same Hebrew root as the word 'end' (Hebrew, *qets* or *qatsah*. *Young's Analytical Concordance*). The Hebrew culture is set within the agrarian cycle, and the end of the cycle of seasons is the summer. The summer is the end of the season of growth and much gets burnt up and dies in the heat. It is not the end in the literal sense, but the end that means there is a new beginning that will follow. For this reason the Jewish New Year begins at the end of the summer season.

W.E.Vine (*Expository Dictionary of New Testatment Words*, Zondervan: 1940) translates '*telos*' in Romans 10:4 as 'the final issue or result of a state or process'. It seemed to be better understood that 'Christ is the *goal* of the law'. Paul explains in Gal 3:24, 'So the law was put in charge *to lead us to Christ* that we might be justified by faith', rather like a school teacher is no longer needed once maturity is reached. That means that the Messiah is the whole *aim* of the law. Amplifying the Hebrew word Torah is another word from the same root, "Yarah", meaning 'to shoot (as with an arrow), so as to hit the target'. The aim of Torah is to direct us to its target – the Messiah. The law has not been abandoned by God; otherwise we would not have known sin.

Paul also writes to the Galatians (3:22), 'But the Scripture declares that the whole world is a prisoner of sin, so that what was promised, being given through faith in Jesus Christ, might be given to those who believe.' The Scripture that Paul refers to here is the Hebrew Scripture, the New Testament not having been formed. 'What was promised' refers to God's covenant promise to Abraham which he has not broken.

The law still has a purpose and that is to lead us to Christ. To abandon that law given at Sinai would be to take away the very covenant which was designed to lead unbelievers to the Messiah. Paul concludes, 'Is the law, therefore, opposed to the promises of God? Absolutely not!' (Gal 3:21).

Paul also gives us a 'before and after' comparison. '*Before* this faith came, we were held prisoners by the law, locked up until faith should be revealed. So the law was put in charge *to lead us to Christ*' (Gal 3:23, 24). As he had already said, 'the law . . . was added [to the Abrahamic covenant] because of transgressions until the Seed to whom the promises referred had come' (Gal 3:19). But, *after*, to those who come to know Jesus Christ as Messiah and Saviour, Paul says, 'Now that faith has come, we are no longer under the supervision [custodian or guard] of the law' (3:25). Without the law, we would not know sin. Paul said, 'I would not have known what sin was except through the law. For I would not have known what coveting really was if the law had not said, "Do not covet"' (Rom 7:7). God is hardly likely to remove the very covenant that makes us realise that we need a Saviour. But once we have found the Saviour we are not under the condemnation of the law, 'because through Christ Jesus the law of the Spirit of life set me free from the law of sin and death' (Rom 8:2).

I raise these points about the law, because it can be so confusing to read one direction of argument concerning the law and then, elsewhere, find the opposite apparently being said.

The question to ask is: 'To whom is the writer addressing the words?' and 'What is the situation he is addressing?' If we trust the law to justify and to save, then, in that respect, the law is obsolete (Heb 8:13). If we attempt to nullify the law by our faith then the answer comes back, 'Not at all! Rather we uphold the law' (Rom 3:31).

Still with Romans 9–11

I suggest that the reader takes a moment to read Chapters 9–11. There are still verses that make me stop and think whether I have understood them correctly. Again, the stand that I have taken is that God has *not* finished with Israel.

As you read, you will find the fishplates still holding the track of Paul's argument together: 'What then shall we say . . .?' (9:14), 'What if . . .?' (9:22), 'What then shall we say?' (9:30), 'How, then ... .?' (10:14), 'But not all . . .' (10:16), 'Again I ask . . .' (10:19), 'I ask then . . .' (11:1), 'Again I ask . . .' (11:11), 'Consider therefore . . .' (11:22), 'Therefore . . .' (12:1).

Chapter 10

THE ALLEGORY OF THE OLIVE TREE

Earlier, I made the analogy of a motorway contraflow down which lane is the only way to find the promises. When we Gentiles come to faith, we cross over into the contraflow lane, out of the peoples of the world lane who are travelling in the wrong direction, and join faithful Israel and the Jewish believers who were first in the contraflow *Promise* lane.

Paul did not have a motorway from which to draw analogies. He described Israel as a cultivated olive tree (11:24) drawn from Jeremiah, 'The Lord called you a thriving olive tree with fruit beautiful in form' (Jer 11:16). The olive tree is like the *Promise* lane. As Paul alludes earlier in chapter 11, the olive tree is the believing remnant of Israel, 'So too, at the present time there is a remnant chosen by grace.' (Rom 11:5). As we have seen, a word study on the remnant is very important in the understanding of our relationship with Israel. It is the remnant that have crossed over into the *Promise* contraflow lane.

Continuing with the olive tree analogy, Paul tells us that the natural branches are also Israel (11:17, 24) and the root of the olive tree he described as 'holy' (11:16b). The root is the patri-archs, Abraham, Isaac, Jacob and David (David, as we have seen is one of the patriarchs, Acts 2:29), for Israel is 'loved on account of the patriarchs' (Rom 11:28). It is through that line the blessing to all peoples flows (Gen 12:3). Hebrews Chapter 11 describes the names of some of those who are part of the stock of the olive tree. How else could there be a list of the faithful men and women from the Hebrew Scriptures unless they had believed God and unless their faith had been 'credited . . . as righteousness' (Rom 4:3–5). Into this stock of Abraham, Isaac, Jacob and David, the Messiah came, Jesus of Nazareth. He is the 'shoot [that] will come up from the stump of Jesse; from his roots a Branch will bear fruit' (Isa 11:1).

Through faith in him, the 'Old Testament' characters who appear in the New Testament, Simeon, Anna and John the Baptist, flourished in the natural olive tree that is Israel. The twelve Apostles and the first Jewish disciples were grafted, like natural branches into their own natural olive tree. They joined the believing remnant of Israel, maybe even up to 18 years before Cornelius and his household became the first wild olive branches recorded specifically in the New Testament to be grafted into the cultivated olive tree (Acts 10). He joined those Gentiles in the Old Testament recorded as being grafted in, as we have seen in the genealogy of Jesus, in Matthew 1.

God had not replaced Israel. Quite the opposite. He had *kept* Israel because the remnant kept faith. Into believing Israel, we are grafted as Gentiles.

Were we to be in any doubt, Paul outlines seven examples of restoration concerning Israel (11:12ff). Their transgression (that is Israel's failure as a nation to accept the Messiah), he contrasts with the promise of fulness (11:12). Their rejection he contrasts with the promise of acceptance (11:15), their being broken off (the natural olive tree), with the promise of being grafted in (11:23–24), experiencing a hardening in part, with the promise of being saved (11:25–26), being godless, with the promise of their sins being taken away (11:26–27), being at present enemies of the gospel, with the truth that they are loved on account of the patriarchs (11:28), being disobedient, with the promise of receiving mercy (11:31–32). If we summarised these they would read: the promise of fulness (11:12), acceptance (11:15), being grafted in again (11:23–24), saved (11:26), their sins taken away (11:27), loved (11:28), receiving mercy (11:32). Some restoration!

By contrast, Paul speaks to us Gentiles (11:13). We are likened to a wild olive shoot grafted in to the natural olive tree (e.g. 11:17, 24). We only share the nourishing sap (17), because it is the root that supports us (18). The Greek word for 'support' (bastazo), means 'bear', 'carry', 'lift up' or 'support'. Paul is saying something extraordinary. It is the holy root of the patriarchs and remnant of Israel into whom we are grafted that supports the church! That turned my theology of the church upside down! Such is the Gentile dominance of the church that I have never dreamt that the believing remnant of Israel, past and present (who are now called Messianic Jews, Jewish Christians or Hebrew Christians), actually carried or supported the church! If anything, I had the notion that Israel was the seed from which the church grew. The seed can die naturally as seeds do and the plant makes its own rooting system. But it is described as a root and nothing can live if the root dies.

Paul continues: we are holy (only) because the root is holy (16). We owe our salvation to Israel, for salvation has come to us because of their disobedience (11). The riches of salvation is a result of their loss (12). Their rejection enabled our reconciliation (15). We were grafted into a community that already existed.

Contrasting Paul's promises of the restoration of Israel, he gives seven warnings to the Gentile Church. Do not boast over the rejected branches of Israel (18). Do not be arrogant (20), (rather) be afraid (20). Consider the kindness and sternness of God (22). Do not be ignorant (25). Do not be conceited (25). Have not these correctives been needed during the 2,000 years of church history which has been so sadly marred by anti-Semitism and persecution of the Jewish people? Finally, do not forget your Hebrew roots in Israel – more commonly referred to as "Jewish roots" (implied by all these warnings).

By now the pendulum of emphasis on the Jewishness of my faith had swung so far that I was beginning to question how I related as a Gentile Christian to my roots. Still those doubts nagged that too much hung on the one analogy of the church being likened to an olive tree, even though it is the second most expansive after the body of Christ analogy given in 1 Corinthians 12. I look at these in the next chapter.

Chapter 11

CITIZENSHIP WITH ISRAEL

The olive tree analogy in Romans 11 seemed clear, but was I to trust in just one, or were there any other analogies that could explain my relationship as a Gentile to those believing Israelites who were already in the *Promise* lane?

I cannot now remember the occasion, but I re-read Ephesians 2 from verse 11 onwards and found, 'Therefore remember that formerly you who are Gentiles by birth and called "uncircumcised" by those who call themselves "the circumcision" [ie the Jewish believers] . . . remember that at that time you [still addressing Gentiles] were separate from Christ, excluded from citizenship in Israel and foreigners to the covenants of the promise, without hope and without God in the world.'

Contrast that state of separation with all the advantages that Paul cites as belonging to the Jews, 'they have been entrusted with the very words of God . . .' (Rom 3:2) and '. . . Theirs is the adoption as sons; theirs the divine glory, the covenants, the receiving of the law, the temple worship and the promises. Theirs are the patriarchs, and from them is traced the human ancestry of Christ' (Rom 9:4–5).

So, if I were an unbelieving *Gentile* I would be separate from Christ (that I knew), and excluded from citizenship in Israel. I was at that time reading the RSV and the word 'citizenship' is translated 'commonwealth'. As a member of the British Commonwealth and having travelled to other parts of the Commonwealth, I found the picture vivid. Just imagine what a British passport and visa must have meant (some decades ago) to someone oppressed by adverse circumstances in one part of the Commonwealth, who could therefore settle in another Commonwealth country as though born there! Paul is saying that I had been born into the commonwealth of Israel with all the riches of their inheritance. Further on in Ephesians 2, Paul says, 'Consequently, you [Gentiles] are no longer foreigners and aliens, but *fellow-citizens* with God's people and [using yet another metaphor] members of God's household' (2:19). I was a foreigner to the covenants of promise. It was not Israel who were foreigners, but I had been the foreigner. How upside down I had made everything! It was I who had to be 'brought near through the blood of Christ', it was I who had been 'far away' (2:13).

Remembering the circumstances of my coming to faith, I could identify so intimately with Paul's words, 'He [Jesus] came and preached peace to you who were far away and peace to those who were near' (2:17). I did not need reminding how far away I had been from the love of God in Jesus the Messiah. I had belonged to the 'other sheep that are *not* of this sheep pen', spoken of by the Good Shepherd in John 10:16 where he said, 'I must bring them also. They too will listen to my voice, and there shall be one flock and one shepherd.' Gentiles are described, therefore, as those who 'were far away' and 'sheep that are *not* of this sheep pen', whereas 'those who were near' and 'this sheep pen', speaks of his people the Jews.

The letter to the Ephesians continues, 'For he himself is our peace, who has made the two one and has destroyed the barrier, the dividing wall of hostility'(2:14). Here were the two distinctly different peoples united in Jesus, Jew and Gentile. In the Messiah, I, as a Gentile believer, remain Gentile, and the Jewish believer remains Jewish. I had become one with them, grafted into them, becoming a fellow citizen in their already existing commonwealth. Little wonder Paul reminded me not to be arrogant!

Metaphor after metaphor!

Paul draws on other metaphors describing believing Gentiles, 'Consequently, you are no longer foreigners and aliens, but fellow-citizens with God's people and members of God's household, built on the foundation of the apostles and prophets, with Christ Jesus himself as the chief cornerstone' (Eph 2:19–20). Picture upon picture, metaphor upon metaphor! Clearly what is built comes *after* what is laid as a foundation. Paul explains that the foundation is laid first upon the Jewish apostles and the Hebrew prophets. How could I have ever been persuaded that it was the New Testament prophets that were foundational to the church? It only required a quick look at the New Testament references to the prophets to see that 'prophets' virtually always refers to the 'Old Testament' prophets unless direct reference is made to members of the church who have a prophetic ministry such as Agabus (Acts 11:28). See, for instance, Peter's second sermon, in Solomon's Colonnade in the Temple area. He demonstrates how Jesus fulfilled what was foretold through all the prophets (Acts 3:18), how 'He must remain in heaven until the time comes for God to restore everything, as he promised long ago through his holy prophets' (3:21) and continues, 'Indeed, all the prophets from Samuel on, as many as have spoken, have foretold these days' (3:24). Here is the emphasis, 'And you [Israel, from verse 12] are *heirs* of the prophets and of the covenant God made with your fathers . . .' (3:25).

The Church is built upon the apostles and prophets. The foundations laid indicate the shape of the building. To suppose that these prophets were *New* Testament prophets would mean that the Church is built on the office of those with a prophetic ministry where only two or three should speak and what is said has to be weighed, or tested, carefully (1 Cor 14:29) in case it is wrong – not to mention that what is prophesied is only 'in part' (1 Cor 13:9).

Please do not misunderstand; I am all for prophecy. We are to desire the gift of prophecy (1 Cor 14:1) and be eager to prophesy (14:39) and are certainly not to treat prophecies with contempt (1 Thess 5:20), but to build a church on such a New Testament spiritual gift is not what I believe Paul had in mind. The words of the prophets in the Hebrew Scriptures were canonical in that they became the Scriptures. Certainly their words were to be tested (Dt 13:1–5 and 18:20–22), but where in the "Old" Testament were the prophets told that they would only prophesy in part?

Jesus came to fulfil the Law and the Prophets (Matt 5:17) and, by saying that 'Everything must be fulfilled that is written about me in the Law of Moses, the Prophets and the Psalms' (Lk 24:44), is he not affirming the veracity of the prophets? Paul does also when he writes of the Hebrew Scriptures, 'All Scripture is God-breathed . . .' (2 Tim 3:16). If the Church is built upon the *New* Testament prophets, then one can only suppose that God has finished with Israel and that all that the Hebrew prophets have said can be written off together with Israel. This has huge implications for the Church, for without the foundation of what the Hebrew (Old Testament) prophets have spoken, we will be tempted to introduce our own prophets and take *their* word as gospel concerning circumstances in the end times and the return of the Lord Jesus Christ.

So, it was clear to me that despite what certain commentaries were saying, the foundation on which we are built is made up of the apostles and the prophets of old, with Messiah Jesus as the chief cornerstone (Eph 2:20).

So we are 'heirs together with Israel' (Eph 3:6). 'Heirs' indicates an inheritance, and the inheritance was theirs first. We are also 'members together of one body' (3:6), and to be a member of something there has to be an existing membership, and Gentiles were not the founder members! Finally we are described as 'sharers together in the promise in Christ Jesus' (3:6).

There is one more picture of our relationship as Gentiles to the believing Israel and Jewish people from Paul's letter to the Galatians, 'If you belong to Christ, then you are Abraham's seed, and heirs according to the promise' (Gal 3:29). This is confirmed in Romans:

> 'Therefore, the promise [that word again!] comes by faith, so that it may be by grace and may be guaranteed to all Abraham's offspring – not only those who are of the law but also to those who are of the faith of Abraham. He is the father of us all. As it is written: "I have made you a father of many nations"' (Rom 4:16,17).

So I was not merely a wild olive branch grafted into a natural olive tree, but I was also a fellow citizen with God's people. I was a member of God's household (the remnant of Israel who remained faithful was God's household) and I was an heir together with Israel, a member of one body and a sharer together in the promise in the Messiah, Christ Jesus, with Abraham as my father. In every analogy, Israel was called first.

Had God finished with Israel? The question now seemed absurd, especially when seen in the light of Paul's categorical exclamations, 'By no means' (Rom 11:1, NIV, RSV), 'I cannot believe it' (NEB), 'Certainly not!' (GNB, AMP, Phillips), 'God forbid' (AV, RV), 'Of course not' (Jerusalem), 'May it never be!' (NASB). I could now take these words at face value, for what other way would Paul have had me take them?

'All Israel will be saved'

Romans 11:26 was the verse that caused me the greatest difficulty. It obviously does not refer to the Church, because the

Church is saved already. As to what the verse means – in one sense I would love the reader to receive the answer from the Lord. It was because I was so committed to salvation only in Jesus Christ that I could not see how God could then save a nation of people and not overturn the *one* way that he promised of coming to him, that is, through individual repentance and a personal commitment to Jesus as Lord. The Jewish people *had* to hear and we *had* to go and tell them the good news (10:14, 15).

The principle that I had been discovering was that 'Israel is Israel is Israel!' and that God had *not* finished with Israel. Furthermore, there was only one gospel, and Scripture was the best source in explaining Scripture.

So, with those principles I came back to this troublesome and yet staggering promise, 'all Israel will be saved'. The NIV cross references this verse to Isaiah 45:17, 'But Israel will be saved by the Lord with an everlasting salvation; you will never be put to shame or disgraced, to ages everlasting.' So Paul was merely reiterating what had already been promised concerning Israel. The New Covenant with both the house of Israel and the house of Judah (all Israel) in Jeremiah 31:31–34 had also stated the promise, '. . . they will all know me, from the least . . . to the greatest,' declares the Lord, 'For I will forgive their wickedness and will remember their sins no more'. Indeed, Paul quotes from this in his development of this future promise, 'The deliverer will come from Zion; he will turn godlessness away from Jacob. And this is my covenant with them when I take away their sins' (Rom 11:26–27, recalling Isa 59:20–21 and 27:9).

God used these verses for me in a mighty way. I was gravely troubled by Israeli secularism. I would wince as I saw Israeli soldiers treat Palestinians in a violent manner and *vice versa*. My point is not that Israel usually gets a bad press, rather that I was seeing godlessness in Israel, in whatever manner it was presented. Somehow I could not relate to the seamy side of a secular twentieth century state grappling with issues of law and order in a similar way to many Western countries. It made me doubt that I was seeing a work of God in the return of the Jewish people to the land of Israel. But, in these verses (11:26–27), Paul is saying that it is *godlessness* that the deliverer will drive out. I believed that God was saying to me that I will *see* godlessness in Jacob (Israel) that will need driving out, whether in the land of Israel or world-wide in the diaspora and that he has covenanted to do just that. How utterly amazing that at a future date, he will come and we will see a people transformed by the saving grace of the Messiah!

No longer was this second-hand opinion, for the conviction had now become mine. I had to learn not to let the media dictate my interpretation of present-day Israel, but allow God's word to interpret it for me.

By allowing Scripture to explain Scripture, I found that the promise, 'all Israel will be saved', parallels Zechariah's prophecy (3:9), 'and I will remove the sin of this land in a single day.' The problem had been my faith. Did I *really* believe that God would one day save Israel?

Clearly Paul was expounding what had already been said of Israel in the Hebrew Scriptures. Now I could see that God had *not* rejected Israel, nor the Jewish people whom he loves. Now it became possible to go back and read these prophetic Scriptures concerning their future with a confidence that I had not previously known. In chapter 15 we shall look at some of the promises concerning her restoration.

But first, I would ask the reader these questions, 'Has this exegesis of Romans shed a different light upon the connection that the Church has with believing Jewish people?' and 'Have these Scriptures gained new integrity?'

Are you with me so far? If you are not, you may find it helpful to write down what your objections are. There is no point in going further yet, because the way we meditate and receive God's word is like chewing on and digesting meat, not like drinking milk, as that is pre-digested, for Paul desires that we eat the solid food of God's word (1 Cor 3:2). If eating fish is acceptable as a similar illustration, then we cannot go on eating if we have a fishbone stuck in our throats! Similarly, if there is an issue that this has raised that has got 'stuck in your throat', then all that will happen is that you cannot eat any more until the bone is removed.

I do hope that the next chapter will be of help in removing any 'fish bones'. This thesis, that God has *not* finished with Israel, began as a hypothesis and has not developed without struggle; and the next chapter may be none too soon in coming as it tackles some of the tricky questions that might begin with the words: 'Yes, but . . .!'

Chapter 12

'YES, BUT . . . !'

Problematic verses had each, for me, acted rather like lenses in a pair of glasses, and as each thin lens on interpretation was added to the frame of my world view concerning Israel and the Jewish people, so each lens had darkened my understanding. I do not believe that I have understood more than a little, 'For we know in part . . . we see but a poor reflection as in a mirror' (1 Cor 13:9, 12). The substantive teaching of the New Testament however, the gospel priority that Jesus and the Apostles had to 'the Jew first', and Paul's teaching in Romans had led me to see that I must tackle these 'yes, but . . .' verses from a different starting point. I have mentioned a few problem verses in the previous chapter which kept coming back to me and made me think my theory was wrong. The way I have tackled them may throw light on the following questions that this theory naturally raises.

Here are some of the counter arguments with which I needed to grapple:

1. Surely the kindom of God has been taken away from Israel? (see Matt 21:43)

Jesus said to his Jewish hearers in the temple courts, 'the kingdom of God will be taken away from you and given to a people who will produce its fruit'. Surely nothing could be clearer!

However, I was helped to look at things a little more closely, remembering some wise words, 'a text without a context is a pretext!' On closer inspection, when Jesus said, 'Therefore I tell *you* . . .' I wondered to whom he was speaking. Looking back in the chapter in Matthew, the context is a challenge, made in the temple by the chief priests and elders of the people, about Jesus' authority to teach (21:23). He turns the question back to the them by asking another question concerning John the Baptist's authority, a question that they could not answer (21:27). Jesus then proceeds to tell them two parables, 'What do *you* think . . .' (28) and 'Listen to another parable . . .' (33). He sums up what he is saying in the verse we are considering, 'Therefore I tell you that the kingdom of God will be taken away from you and given to a people who will produce its fruit' (43). So he is talking to the chief priests and elders of the people, not to Israel as a nation.

Matthew confirms this two verses later, 'When the chief priests and the Pharisees heard Jesus' parables, they knew he was talking about *them*' (21:45). So the kingdom, Jesus says, will be taken from the chief priests and elders of the people, ie the leaders. But who are the people who will bear its fruit to whom Jesus refers? Again, looking back to the context, we see that Matthew has already mentioned the people. In trying to answer Jesus' question as to where John the Baptist's authority had come from, the religious leaders are recorded as discussing it among themselves, 'If we say, "from heaven", he will ask, "Then why didn't you believe him?" But if we say, "From men" – we are afraid of the *people*, for they all hold that John was a prophet' (21:25–26). Concluding this encounter with the chief priests and Pharisees, Matthew writes, 'They looked for a way to arrest him, but they were afraid of the crowd because the people held that he [Jesus] was a prophet' (21:45).

So twice we are told that the leaders were afraid of the people and, in our problem text, it is a people who will produce the fruit of the kingdom of God. It is unlikely to be Gentiles in this instance, because Gentiles are translated 'peoples' or 'nations', and Israel as 'people' or 'nation' singular.

I was persuaded, rather, that Jesus as the Good Shepherd came to care for his flock, as foretold in Ezekiel 34. The Lord declares himself against the shepherds of Israel, 'Woe to the shepherds of Israel who only take care of themselves! . . .' (Ezek 34:2). The chief priests and elders of the people certainly fitted that description. The prophet's message from the Lord concludes, 'You my sheep, the sheep of my pasture, are *people*, and I am your God, declares the Sovereign Lord' (34:31). I believe that the people to whom the kingdom will be given are those from Israel who accept Jesus (or Yeshua) as the Messiah (or Ha Mashiach) and Gentiles who receive their message, the kingdom moving from the leadership who rejected him to the people who receive him.

Finally, the kingdom referred to by Jesus cannot refer to the land of Israel, as the kingdom of God does not equate with the land, otherwise we would have to see the kingdom in territorial terms, rather than the sovereign rule of the King.

2. Surely the New Testament replaces the Old?

We have touched on this in an earlier chapter. The argument might start with Hebrews 7:22, '. . . Jesus has become the guarantee of a better covenant' and 8:6–7,

> . . . the ministry Jesus has received is as superior to theirs as the covenant of which he is mediator is superior to the old one . . . For if there had been *nothing wrong* with that first covenant, no place would have been sought for another.

It seems clear from these and other verses that the New Covenant in the blood of Jesus replaces and does away with the Old Covenant. It is a 'shadow' (Heb 10:1). The conclusion drawn is that there can therefore be no ongoing covenant with Israel since God broke this because of their disobedience.

Remember the theory that God has *not* rejected Israel and *still* keeps his covenants with Israel. Can we see these verses from a different angle? I believe so.

Let's look at Heb 9:1, 'Now the first covenant had regulations for worship and also an earthly sanctuary'. Wait a minute! When referring to the 'first covenant' in these verses, the writer to the Hebrews is actually talking about the Mosaic covenant. The covenant that promises a future to Israel is the Abrahamic covenant, in Gen 12:2–3; 13:15–16; 15:18–21; 17:4–8,19,21; 22:15–18, which was also confirmed with Isaac and Jacob.

As we have already seen, of this covenant, Paul himself says, 'The law [that is the Mosaic covenant spoken of in the Hebrews passages from which I have quoted] . . . *does not set aside* the covenant previously established by God and thus do away with the promise' (Gal 3:17).

At first glance, it appears from the letter to the Hebrews, written to the Hebrew Christians or Messianic believers, that the New Covenant has replaced the Old, whereas actually the writer tells us how superior the New Covenant is when compared with the Mosaic covenant.

3. Doesn't this mean there is a different gospel for the Jews?

No! 'Salvation is found in no-one else, for there is no other name under heaven given to men by which we must be saved' (Acts 4:12) – and Peter was addressing the Sanhedrin. Indeed salvation had come before the New Covenant was given (see Hebrews 11), but now salvation was in Jesus. Paul (Gal 1:8, 9), calls down a curse on anyone, even an angel, who should preach a contrary gospel. In Romans 10:1, and 14–16, he specifically points to Jewish people needing to hear the gospel.

How, then, can they [unsaved Jewish people] call on the one they have not believed in? And how can they believe in the one of whom they have not heard? And how can they hear without someone preaching to them? And how can they preach unless they are sent? As it is written, 'How beautiful are the feet of those who bring good news!' (Rom 10:14–15).

No, there is not another gospel, but there *is* a people (Israel) who have *yet* to turn (in significant numbers) and accept the Lord Jesus as their Saviour (Rom 11:25–29), for the God of Abraham, Isaac and Jacob is still a covenant-keeping God.

4. Surely God no longer distinguishes Jews from Gentiles?

You may be thinking of Paul's teaching, 'There is neither Jew nor Greek, slave nor free, male nor female, for you are all one in Christ Jesus' (Gal 3:28, cf Col 3:11). Surely this means that as far as the gospel is concerned, God does not see Jews as being different from Greeks (Gentiles). If this were so, then from this teaching, there are no males or females either! And why did Wilberforce and others work so tirelessly for so long if there were no slaves! More particularly, the Holy Spirit as the inspirer of Scripture (2 Tim 3:16, 2 Peter 1:21) deemed Jewish people so important that he was the inspiration of an entire letter written to them, the letter to the Hebrews! How could he desire to do that if there were no recognisably Jewish believers?

If we look at the context of Paul's argument in Galatians, it is that we are *all* sons of God '*through faith* in Christ Jesus' (Gal 3:26). In other words, there is no distinction in terms of salvation, whether Jew or Greek, male or female, slave or free, we must *all* come to Jesus Christ *by faith*. He is not writing Jews off as an ethnic group, merely writing off any group which thinks, in respect of faith, it can choose any other way.

Paul, employing the same phraseology, tells us that Jews and Greeks are all baptised into one body (1 Cor 12:13). If Jews are baptised into the body of Christ, they are still reckoned as Jews. Again, a similar phrase comes in Colossians 3:11. The NIV heading is 'Rules for holy living' and includes the 'take off' and 'put on' analogy that Paul employs. The same conclusion can be drawn, that, concerning this rule for holy living, there is no distinction between Jews or Greeks. The Greeks are not thereby written off as an ethnic group, so why should the Jews?

In Ephesians 2:14, Paul says that Jesus 'is our peace, who has made the two *one* and has destroyed the barrier, the diving wall of hostility'. This is quite literally the wall that prevented Gentiles from entering the Temple itself. Thus Jewish people and Gentiles were separated by a barrier. In Jesus, we are made one. Do I cease to be Gentile in being made one with the Jews? Of course not! Then if I do not, why should believing Jewish people cease to be identifiably Jewish?

5. Surely the Church is now the 'Israel of God'?

This title for the Church is based on Gal 6:16 'Peace and mercy to all who follow this rule, even to *the Israel of God'*. From this we get the idea that the Church is the 'New Israel'.

This verse, out of at least 70 references to Israel, is the only reference in the New Testament that, at first sight appears to suggest that the church is now the 'New Israel'.

We are dealing with a singular exception, and the key principle for understanding Scripture must be that the plain teaching of the Bible should explain the obscure and not the other way around! Here then is an obscure text. If the term 'Israel' is employed to replace the word 'church' in any other verse in the New Testament then the context makes no sense at all. Putting this verse in context, Paul is writing to warn the Galatians about the Judaisers, 'Those who want to make a good impression outwardly are trying to compel you to be circumcised' (Gal 6:12). Clearly it was the Gentile believers who were being pressurised to be circumcised as Jews, for, by definition, Jews had already been circumcised. Paul continues in the next verse, speaking again of the Judaisers,

> 'Not even those who are circumcised [Jews] obey the law, yet they want you [Gentiles] to be circumcised that they may boast about your flesh . . . Neither circumcision nor uncircumcision means anything [when it comes to believing, saving faith – 2:15,16]; what counts is a new creation. Peace and mercy to all who follow this rule, even to the Israel of God' (6:13,15–16).

Paul is simply saying that he wants peace and mercy to both Gentiles, who do *not* need to be circumcised and know it, and Jewish believers (the faithful remnant of Israel), who *have already* been circumcised before their commitment of faith in Yeshua as Messiah. These must learn not to trust that their circumcision has any value as far as salvation is concerned.

Furthermore, Paul, as the apostle to the Gentiles (Rom 11:13, Gal 1:16), wanted to teach the Churches in Galatia (Gal 1:2) about justification by faith (Gal 2:16). He contrasts this justification that comes by faith with the Judaisers who wanted the Gentiles to *lose* the freedom they had gained through their new-found faith in the Messiah, and return to a perverse legalism. Besides, why would the apostle want to muddle his readers by changing the name of the 'church' back to the collective noun 'Israel' in 6:16, the very source of the problem that he has been at pains to identify?

Finally, the Greek word for '*even*' to the Israel of God, is '*kai*' and the standard translation in the New Testament of that word is 'and' (NEB, NASB). The verse would then read '*and* to the Israel of God', pointing to an additional (and different) group of people. Surely that different group are the believing Jews who had *already* been circumcised.

The 'Israel of God', far from being the church, is therefore more likely to refer to the believing Jews and the faithful remnant of Israel, the natural branches *already* grafted back into their own olive tree (Rom 11:23). It is another collective noun for believing Israel and Jewish people, as are the terms 'God's people' and 'members of God's household' used by Paul to describe the Jewish believers (Eph 2:19). It is *they* who needed reminding that a new creation is what counts.

6. We belong to the Jerusalem that is from above

You might want to quote from Paul's allegory concerning Hagar and Sarah in Galatians 4:21–5:1, where the covenant at Sinai is cast in such bad light as to suggest that we can 'get rid of' it (to use Paul's terminology applied to the slave woman in verse 30). In contrast, we believers have a heavenly Jerusalem from which we are born (26).

From this 'figurative' allegory, some would deduce that God has rejected 'the present city of Jerusalem' (25) and replaced it with the 'Jerusalem . . . above'. Is this not what the writer to the Hebrews is saying, 'But you have come to Mount Zion, to the heavenly Jerusalem, the city of the living God' (Heb 12:22)?

In Galatians, Paul addresses those 'who want to be under the law' (4:21), that is the 'foolish Galatians' (3:1), who are being pressurised by the Judaisers to be circumcised (5:2). Paul writes 'figuratively' (4:24) about two covenants, the Mosaic covenant and the New Covenant. The 'present city of Jerusalem' in Paul's analogy are the Jews 'who rely on observing the law' (3:10), and he emphasises that 'no-one is justified before God by the law' (3:11). Because there are Galatians who *want* to be under the law, he then describes the New Covenant, the Jerusalem from above, as being 'free, and she is our mother' (4:26). It is not that one Jerusalem replaces the other, but that we as believers are born from the Jerusalem above (figuratively, the New Covenant) and that we are free from the condemnation of the law of legalism represented by the 'present city of Jerusalem' (Gal 5:1, Rom 8:1–4).

There are still other verses that appear to give substance to the notion that God has rejected Israel in favour of the Church. Try approaching these verses from the viewpoint of this study: 'Did God reject his people? By no means!' (Rom 11:1), as well as considering the context of the verse, to whom it is addressed and the influence of the presenting problem. While it is fresh in your mind, note the verses that for you suggest God *has* finished with his people Israel, and then come back to them after you have read on.

Chapter 13

SEPARATING FROM OUR JEWISH ROOTS

I was asking the question, 'If the substance of this book is correct, then why is it that the early Gentile believers did not appreciate their Jewish roots?' If God had *not* rejected Israel, but had a glorious purpose for the world through Israel, how could such an enormous error creep into the Church?

It was clear to me from reading the book of Acts, that as Luke chooses to present the mission of the Church in the way that he does, then, until the conversion of the Roman centurion, Cornelius, all the believers were either Jewish by birth or were already proselytes (those who converted to Judaism). Therefore the early Church up to that point was entirely Jewish and would have seen themselves as a group within established Judaism. In the same way as within the Church of England there are varieties of churchmanship – liberal, evangelical, charismatic, Anglo Catholic and so on, so within Judaism. There were already within the establishment Scribes, Pharisees, Sadducees, Herodians (and we also know that there were Essenes), and now there were Messianic Jews as well. Various factors began to distance the early Jewish believers from the Judaism of Jesus' day.

The first factor was obviously the influence of the unbelieving Jewish leadership who continually tried to expel the believing Jews from the synagogues, mockingly referring to them as a 'Nazarene sect' (Acts 24:5). They wanted to marginalise this new sect.

Seeds of separation were present from the moment in Acts 6:1 when Grecian Jews and Hebraic Jews had to cope with a pastoral problem within the church. The Grecian Jews were those whose first language was Greek and who may well have come from the Diaspora and lived away from Jerusalem which had the sacrificial system of the temple and the priesthood. They had already accepted that they could not take literally the commandments relating to the temple sacrifices, but saw these completed in Jesus. The Hebraic Jews on the other hand had a framework of observant Judaism within the establishment of Israel. Stephen, the Greek-speaking Jew, could say that 'the Most High does not live in houses made by men' (Acts 7:48) and then quoted from Isa 66. I wonder if it was 'when they heard this' (54) that, responsible as they were for the temple, they stoned him? In Acts 8:1, it is the Hebrew Apostles who are allowed to remain in Jerusalem but the rest are scattered. Already a distinction was being made.

Once Cornelius and his household had received the Messiah (Acts 10:45), it was clear to the Apostles that Gentiles could become believers too. Some Jewish believers (the Judaisers) tried to make Gentiles keep the law. Acts 15 illustrates the big debate, 'Can Gentiles become Christians without first becoming Jews?' The answer was a categorical 'Yes!' Gentiles did *not* need to become Jews in order to be Christians! (Acts 15:24–29). How interesting that Gentiles have turned that around and now ask, 'Can Jews become Christians without giving up their Jewishness and becoming Gentiles?'

The process of winning and integrating Gentiles further angered the Jewish leaders. They saw the 'warm fringe' of the synagogues, which included many Gentile God-fearers, joining this new movement without having to undergo circumcision, the serious sign of commitment to Judaism. This created jealousy (Acts 13:45). Thus mainstream Judaism and the Messianic movement were further distanced from each other.

It was at the largely Gentile church at Antioch that the term 'Christians' was coined as a nickname, based on 'Christos', the Greek word for the Messiah. The international language of the day was Greek and not Hebrew, and the New Testament Scriptures were written in Greek. This in itself separated the language continuation of what would now be called 'Old' and 'New' Testaments, the Hebraisms of the New Testament world-view being thus obscured by Greek language and expression.

When Jerusalem was surrounded in AD 68 and the Temple subsequently destroyed in AD 70, the Jewish believers in the Church recognised the words of Jesus in Luke 21:20,

> 'When you see Jerusalem being surrounded by armies, you will know that its desolation is near. Then let those who are in Judea flee to the mountains, let those in the city get out, and let those in the country not enter the city.'

Tradition has it that they fled to Pella and not one was killed (Eusebius, H.E. III.5.3). For this they were naturally seen as traitors and further alienated from mainstream Judaism.

In time, Gentiles began to outnumber the Jewish believers. The passages in Scripture castigating the Jewish leaders and Judaisers (Matt 23; 1 Thess 2:14–16) were increasingly interpreted as condemnation of all that was Jewish.

With the destruction of the Temple and the Dispersion of the Jews, the question arose, 'How could Judaism survive without a Temple?' The synagogue had already provided the answer, especially for those Jews who lived away from Jerusalem, replacing 'Biblical Judaism', the priesthood and Temple, with the Rabbi and 'rabbinical Judaism'. This form of rabbinical Judaism, with its emphasis on rabbinical law, led to the Messianic believers distancing themselves from traditional Judaism, as Jesus the Messiah had freed them from legalism and bondage to the law.

By this time, the Jewish authorities had added a prayer for daily synagogue worship, 'For the apostates let there be no hope and may . . . the sectarians . . . perish in a moment'. This made it impossible for Jewish believers to be open in their attendance and pressurised them to leave the synagogues.

Eventually the Church began to use for herself the title 'Israel'. Early Church fathers, notably, Ignatius of Antioch, Justin Martyr, John Chrysostom and Marcion, were writing vitriolic anti-Jewish statements and, later, Martin Luther did too. (See *'Our Father Abraham'* Marvin Wilson, Eerdmans, 1989 chapter 7). Because Jews had rejected Jesus, the argument went, then why should the Church feel any indebtedness to Jews? Was it not the Jews who crucified Christ? Was not the opprobrium correct and summed up in Paul's words,

> . . .the Jews, who killed the Lord Jesus and the prophets and also drove us out. They displease God and are hostile to all men in their effort to keep us from speaking to the Gentiles so that they may be saved. In this way they always heap up their sins to the limit. The wrath of God has come upon them at last (1 Thess 2:14b–16).

(Yet we remind ourselves in the Nicene Creed, 'For our sake he was crucified under Pontius Pilate', a Gentile, ASB.)

The process was almost complete. The Messianic believers had started within Judaism but were now being forced to find a distinct identity outside mainstream Judaism. The Bar Kochba Revolt of AD 132 further widened the divide between the two communities. Bar Kochba was hailed as the Messiah by Rabbi Akiva, and the Jewish believers had to withdraw their support from the his leadership of opposition to Rome because they believed Jesus to be the Messiah and consequently they were seen as complete heretics. The opposition of the Jewish establishment to the believers became violent and this sealed the complete separation.

The Gentile Church, though persecuted by Rome, failed to

understand Jewish believers who retained their Jewishness, and the Messianic movement now separated from both Church and Judaism.

Perhaps the watershed in the process of the Church separating from its Jewish roots came soon after the Roman Emperor Constantine became a Christian in AD 312. He passed various anti-Semitic laws. These were resisted actively by the Jewish community. Furthermore, worship on the Sabbath was banned. Jewish festivals were replaced by Christianised pagan ones; Passover was replaced by Easter, Sukkot by Harvest and Hannukah by Christmas. All the time it forced Christians to sever their roots from their Jewish heritage, and Messianic Jews from their own community. Christians who had up to this time been persecuted, now turned on the Jewish community who had largely escaped unharmed.

Not only had the Jewish people rejected the believing remnant from within their midst, but the Church that grew from the Messianic believers became distinctly anti-Semitic.

Christianity was adopted as the official religion of the Roman Empire, the Church grew enormously, and sadly anti-Semitism increased as well. A theology had to be worked out as to why God should reject the Jews so decisively by allowing the destruction of the Temple and the Diaspora. The answer was perceived to be that God had rejected Israel and transferred all the promises to the Church. Thus the Church 'replaced' Israel.

The Church was now overwhelmingly Gentile and could outvote the Jewish believers. Indeed at the Council of Nicea, Jewish believers were forbidden to attend. How incredible that our Nicene Creed had no input from those with a Jewish, and therefore Hebrew, background to the Bible!

This separation, therefore, meant that the Messianic Jews were rejected by *both* the Church *and* the Synagogue. The former lost the richness and fullness spoken of by Paul in Romans 11, and the latter lost the very group that the Messiah had sent to reach them first.

We have inherited the misunderstandings of the past. I had a terrible shock as I first encountered writings of certain Early Church Fathers. For instance, Chrysostom wrote in one of his sermons concerning the Jews,

'They sacrificed their sons and daughters to devils: they outraged nature and overthrew from their foundations the laws of relationships. They are become worse than the wild beasts, and for no reason at all, with their own hands they murder their offspring, to worship the avenging devils who are the foes of our life . . . they are lustful, rapacious, greedy, perfidious bandits . . . inveterate murderers, destroyers, men possessed by the devil . . . debauchery, drunkenness have given them the manners of a pig and the lusty goat. They know only one thing, to satisfy their gullets, get drunk, to kill and maim one another' (Chrystostom's Sermons as quoted by Parkes, 'The Conflict of the Church and Synagogue', pp 163–164).

Perhaps one further quote from the Reformation and from Martin Luther himself might suffice, indicating his frustration at the Jewish community who would not receive the Lord,

'Burn their synagogues and schools; what will not burn, bury with earth, that neither stone nor rubbish remain. In like manner break into and destroy their homes. Take away their prayer books and Talmuds, in which there is nothing but godlessness, lies, cursing and swearing. Forbid their Rabbis to teach, on pain of life or limb . . . If I had power over them I would assemble their most prominent men and demand that they prove that we Christians do not worship God, under penalty of having their tongues torn out through the back of the neck' (Stevens 'Strife Between Brothers', Olive Press, St Albans: 1979, p 34).

I read the book from which I have just quoted, on a train journey up to London and became aware of a tremendous fear within me of getting caught up in this conflict of church and synagogue, of the Jews and world history. There was enough conflict in the world without willingly exploring this enormous sadness. 'Peace at any price' would probably be my motto, but I was recognising a strand in my own theology that had received this rejection of God's chosen people. I had no option but to keep searching. Had God finished with Israel?

Part II

EXPLORING AN APPLICATION

Chapter 14

AN INTRODUCTION TO PROPHECY

So far we have been laying foundations, particularly those in the ministry of Jesus, the covenants and the priority seen in Acts and Romans. As far as Biblical prophecy was concerned, I really had to start all over again. You have seen the journey that I was making and looking back over the past chapters, it seems tortuously slow!

You may know the experience of a Christian quoting a verse from the Hebrew (Old Testament) Scriptures as meaning something to them and yet the very same verse says something very different to you. How then should we start in our understanding, especially concerning things yet to come?

For me, Jesus Christ *had* to be the starting point in understanding and testing Biblical prophecy in that he is the Word made flesh (John 1:14); he is God's message in person. In his own words, he came to fulfil the Law and the Prophets (Matt 5:17) and he is 'the prophet who is to come' (Jn 6:14; cf Acts 3:22, quoting Dt 18:15). This meant to me that he would fulfil in his earthly life much of what the prophets foretold and, in his Second Coming, those yet unfulfilled.

I had come to put my trust in him and found his testimony to be true, that he is the Son of God, crucified for our sins, risen and ascended and alive for evermore, and that he has all authority in heaven and earth.

131

Jesus – 'in all the Scriptures'

I had been looking for a handle in terms of the prophetic Scriptures and this was where the journey began. If you have a Bible open, do look with me. The context is the resurrection walk that Jesus made with two disciples, Cleopas and probably his wife (Lk 24:13–35). Interestingly, they might well have been related to the Lord, because in Jn 19:25 it could be inferred that Mary the wife of Clopas was the sister of Mary the mother of Jesus. (The NIV cross references this Clopas to the Cleopas of Luke 24:18.) Whatever the relationship, the event underlines the priority that Jesus gave to his people, even appearing to family and followers rather than the high priests or Pilate. The two disciples did not recognise him and did not understand that he must rise from the dead. He rebuked them, '"How foolish you are, and how slow of heart to believe all that the prophets have spoken!" And beginning with Moses and all the prophets, he explained to them what was said in all the Scriptures concerning himself' (Lk 24:27).

Their problem was that they did not see in their own (Hebrew) Scriptures that the Messiah should suffer. We have no problem with that, for we emphasise and are eternally grateful for the suffering of Christ, and we see his suffering foretold in the Hebrew Scriptures (Tanach), for instance in Psalm 22 and Isaiah 53.

I had come to realise that, for many reasons, my problem was that I did *not* 'believe all that the prophets have spoken!' (Lk 24:25). I was on secure ground concerning his suffering, but was not at all sure about the rest of what the prophets foretold.

So, beginning with Moses and all the Prophets I began a new journey. We do not know what Scriptures Jesus pointed to as he went through the five books of Moses and the Prophets, but every time I would read in the gospels or other books of the New Testament the phrase, 'this was spoken by the prophet . . .'

or 'this fulfilled . . .' I would turn up the cross reference and highlight that verse in the Hebrew Scriptures.

(There are prophecies concerning the Messiah in the *NIV Thompson Chain Reference Bible* [Chain Index 2890] and illustration on page 1511. The NIV has also produced a *New Covenant Prophecy Edition* in which many of the Hebrew Scripture prophecies of the Messiah are set out showing their New Covenant fulfilment.)

The Messiah would be born of a woman. Jesus began with Moses, and the first direct prophecy that I could find concerning the coming of a Messianic figure in the Hebrew Scriptures and declared fulfilled by Jesus in the New Covenant was that the Messiah would be 'the offspring of a woman'. It reads in Genesis 3, 'And I will put enmity between you [the serpent] and the woman [Eve] and between your offspring and hers; he will crush your head, and you will strike his heel' (Gen 3:15). So the Messiah would be 'the seed of a woman'. The narrative accounts of the birth of Jesus go to great lengths to confirm that it was of a woman that Jesus was born. 'She [Mary] gave birth to her firstborn, a son' (Lk 2:7). Paul also confirms this, 'But when the time had fully come, God sent His Son, born of a woman' (Gal:4:4).

We have seen from chapter 4 on the covenants with Israel that this offspring would be of Abraham (Gen 22:18). It would be as well to read the whole of this particular promise of God that follows Abraham's obedience in being willing to sacrifice Isaac:

'I swear by myself, declares the Lord, that because you have done this and not withheld your son, your only son, I will surely bless you and make your descendants as numerous as the stars in the sky and as the sand on the seashore. Your descendants will take possession of the cities of their enemies, and through your *offspring* all nations on earth will be blessed, because you have obeyed me' (Gen 22:16–18).

Again, turn to the New Testament (Acts 3), and Peter says to his hearers who had come running to both him and John, amazed at the healing of the crippled beggar at the Beautiful gate in the temple (Acts 3:25) 'He [God] said to Abraham, "Through your offspring all peoples on earth will be blessed"'. This interpretation is confirmed in Matthew 1:1 and Luke 3:34, where Jesus is recorded as being 'the Son of . . . Abraham'.

The simple exercise of seeing a prophecy and turning back to the Hebrew Scriptures and then checking its New Testament affirmation has had, for me, the effect of strengthening the sense of integrity that there is between both Testaments.

This pattern of investigation repeated itself, so that the next reference shows that the 'offspring' is to be of Isaac.

> The Lord appeared to Isaac and said, ". . . to you and your descendants I will give all these lands and will confirm the oath I swore to your father Abraham. I will make your descendants as numerous as the stars in the sky and will give them all these lands, and through *your offspring* all nations on earth will be blessed" (Gen 26:2–4).

The same promise is repeated to Jacob (Gen 28:13–15).

Jesus may have drawn those two disciples' attention to Numbers 24:17, 'A star will come out of Jacob; a sceptre will rise out of Israel,' and Genesis 49:10, 'The sceptre will not depart from Judah, nor the ruler's staff from between his feet, until he comes to whom it belongs and the obedience of the nations is his'. That 'obedience of the nations' has not yet happened. I was not convinced that Church history had, at any point, led to such obedience and so I was now having to grapple with the thought that Jesus would *yet* rule the nations. More later!

The Messiah would be a prophet like Moses. (Dt 18:15,18–19). In order to limit this chapter, see John 7:14–17, 40–46 and Acts 3:22–26 for the New Testament confirmation that this prophecy speaks of Jesus.

He would be born a King. 'I have installed my King on Zion, my holy hill' (Psalm 2:6) was written around 1,000 years before Jesus was born, and confirmed as pointing to Jesus in the New Testament in Matt 2:2, 'Where is the one who has been born king of the Jews? We saw his star in the east and have come to worship him'. (See also Matt 27:11,37). I have already developed the fulfilment of Jesus' kingship in chapter 4 on the covenants.

The Messiah would be born of a virgin. Writing about 740 years before Jesus was born, Isaiah records, 'Therefore the Lord himself will give you a sign: The virgin will be with child and will give birth to a son, and will call him Immanuel' (Isaiah 7:14. New Testament fulfilment, Matt 1:18–25; Lk 1:26–38).

The Messiah would be born in Bethlehem. Written about 742 years before Jesus was born, 'But you, Bethlehem Ephrathah, though you are small among the clans of Judah, out of you will come for me one who will be ruler over Israel, whose origins are from of old' (Micah 5:2. New Testament fulfilment, Matt 2:1–6; Lk 2:1–20).

The Messiah would be born of the House of David. Written about 600 years before Jesus was born, Jeremiah 23:5 reads: 'The days are coming . . . when I will raise up to David a right-eous Branch [rather like the idea of a 'family tree' – Jesus would be a branch of King David's family], a King who will reign wisely and do what is just and right in the land' (New Testament fulfilment, Lk 3:23, 31).

The Messiah would enter Jerusalem in triumph. Zechariah 9:9. Fulfilled in the New Testament, Matt 21:1–9; Jn 12:12–16.

The Messiah would be rejected by his own people. Written around 740 years before Jesus was born, Isaiah 53:3, 'He was despised and rejected by men, a man of sorrows, and familiar with suffering'. (Also Ps 118:22.) Fulfilled in the New Testament in Matt 26:3–4; John 12:37–43; Acts 4:1–12. Also see John 1:11, 'He came to that which was his own, but his own did not receive him.'

The Messiah would suffer. He would be betrayed by one of his followers (Ps 41:9. See Matt 26:14–16, 47–50; Mk 14:17–21; Lk 22:19–23; John 13:18–19), sold for thirty pieces of silver (Zech 11:12–13. See Matt 26:15, 27:3–10), and the money returned to buy the potter's field (Zech 11:13. See Matt 27:3–10). False witnesses accuse him (Ps 27:12. See Matt 26:60–61). He would be hated without cause (Ps 69:4, 109:3–5. See Jn 15:23–25). He would be tried and condemned (Isa 53:8. See Matt 27:1–2; Lk 23:1–25), be silent before his accusers (Isa 53:7. See Matt 27:12–14, Mk 15:3–4; Lk 23:8–10), be beaten and spat upon (Mic 5:1; Isa 50:6. See Matt 26:67, 27:30; Mk 15:19; Lk 22:63–64 and Jn 19:1–3), and be mocked and taunted (Ps 22:7–8. See Matt 27:39–43; Lk 23:11, 35).

The Messiah would be crucified, 'They have pierced my hands and my feet', written about 1,000 years before Jesus was born (Ps 22:16, also 14,17; and Isa 52:13–14; 53:5. See Matt 27:31,35; Mk 15:20,25; Lk 23:33; Jn 19:23). He would be given gall and vinegar (Ps 69:21. See Jn 19:29), and hear prophetic words repeated in mockery (Ps 22:8. See Matt 27:43). His side would be pierced (Zech 12:10. See Jn 19:34–37), soldiers would cast lots for his clothes (Ps 22:18. See Mk 15:24; Jn 19:24) and none of his bones would be broken (Num 9:12; Ex 12:46; Ps 34:20. See Jn 19:31–37).

The Messiah would die as an offering for sin (Isa 53:5–6,8,10–12. See Jn 1:29; 11:49–52; Acts 10:43, 13:38–39; 1 Cor 15:3, Eph 1:7; 1 Pet 2:24–25; 1 Jn 1:7, 9), and be buried with the rich (Isa 53:9. See Matt 27:57–60). He would be raised from the dead (Ps 16:10; and Isa 53:10b–11a. See Matt 28:1–10; Mk 16:1–14; Lk

24:1–44; Jn 20:1–31; Acts 1:3; 2:22–32; 1 Cor 15:4–8), and would ascend into heaven (Ps 68:18. See Lk 24:50–51; Acts 1–11), and would sit at God's right hand (Ps 110:1. See Mark 16:19; Acts 2:33–36; Heb 1:3; 10:12–13; 1 Peter 3:22).

Conclusion

I did not need convincing that Jesus was indeed the Messiah. The incredible detail of the life, death and exaltation of Jesus Christ prophesied in the Hebrew Scriptures and fulfilment in the New Covenant provided the most amazing evidence possible.

The odds against Jesus fulfilling a mere handful of these prophecies are enormous. It was this accuracy of fulfilment, repeated over and over again by the New Testament writers, that led to the obvious conclusion – that the events prophesied and still *yet* to happen, *will also come about*.

The writer to the Hebrews says, 'Therefore, when Christ came into the world, he said: . . . "Here I am – it is written about me in the scroll – I have come to do your will, O God"' (Heb 10:5,7, quoting Ps 40:7–8). That could well summarise what Jesus may have said to those two disciples along that road to Emmaus.

They ran back to Jerusalem to tell the others, and the risen Jesus appeared to them again and to the Eleven and underlined his message to them, 'Everything must be fulfilled that is written about me in the Law of Moses, the Prophets and the Psalms' (Lk 24:44).

So, for me, the starting point was discovering Jesus in the Hebrew Scriptures.

The second step was now less difficult. In seeing so many of the prophetic statements fulfilled in the birth, life, death and resurrection of the Lord Jesus Christ, it was easier to see that the prophecies that have *yet* to happen are certain to be fulfilled too.

Signs of the coming of the Lord

It has been said of prophecies in the Hebrew Scriptures that they are rather like looking at a distant range of mountains, with the attendant difficulty of distinguishing which are the nearer mountain peaks and which are the farther. So in the Hebrew Scriptures, prophecies are intermingled just as the mountain peaks are in a distant view.

That took me back to the New Covenant prophecies concerning the Messiah's Second Coming with which I was familiar and which are based principally upon the words of Jesus Christ in Matthew 24 and Luke 21.

We have seen some of the peaks in the foreground of prophecy and identified these in the first coming of Jesus. We now turn to the peaks farthest from the prophets' view, his Second Coming.

We come to those passages enshrined in the simple, but profound statement in our Creed, 'We believe . . . he will come again in glory to judge the living and the dead, and his kingdom will have no end' (ASB).

The signs of his coming are numerous. If we return to the motorway analogy, then hazard signs will appear above the road.

These signs will be in the political arena with 'wars and rumours of wars' (Matt 24:6), 'when nation will rise against nation, and kingdom against kingdom' (24:7). We have not been short of these! There will be natural disasters in terms of 'famines' (Matt 24:7) and 'pestilences' (Luke 21:11). He speaks of geological disasters, 'earthquakes' (Matt 24:7), of social disintegration, and the lawlessness, violence, immorality that was prevalent at the time of the flood (Matt 24:37–39). How incredibly reliable are the words of Jesus nearly 2,000 years ago.

He further tells us that there will be phenomena in the religious field of apostasy, that is a recognisably marked falling away of belief in God and the Lord Jesus Christ, 'At that time many

WATCH FOR SIGNS

will turn away from the faith and will betray and hate each other . . .' (Matt 24:10–12).

He describes great evangelistic effort in terms of world mission, 'And this gospel of the kingdom will be preached in the whole world as a testimony to all nations, *and then the end will come*' (Matt 24:14; cf Mark 13:10).

He speaks of a time of great distress (sometimes known as 'tribulation') and specifically relates this to the land of Israel. An 'abomination that causes desolation' in 'the holy place . . . spoken of through the prophet Daniel . . . let those . . . in Judea flee . . .' (Matt 24:15–22).

He warns us that false Christs will appear (Matt 24:23–24) and that the Gentile domination of Jerusalem will be ended (Lk 21:20–21, 24). Whether we agree with the circumstances of that domination ending as it did in the Six-Day War in June 1967, that prophecy, too, has been fulfilled.

In connection with the last days, other passages in the Bible point to further characteristics that we should expect. Daniel mentions that 'Many will go here and there to increase knowledge' (Daniel 12:4), indicating a time of travel and desire for knowledge.

Paul reminds Timothy, in these chilling words,

'But mark this: There will be terrible times in the last days. People will be lovers of themselves, lovers of money, boastful, proud, abusive, disobedient to their parents, ungrateful, unholy, without love, unforgiving, slanderous, without self-control, brutal, not lovers of the good, treacherous, rash, conceited, lovers of pleasure rather than lovers of God – having a form of godliness but denying its power (2 Tim 3:1–5).

There is no need for commentary on these characteristics of our day. If in doubt, read today's newspaper! Do you not recognise many of the warning signs already being fulfilled in our time?

Finally, both Paul and John speak of a future ruler who would be an 'antichrist' ('anti' meaning, not so much 'against', but rather 'instead of' Christ, one who would usurp the sovereignty of Jesus himself (1 Jn 2:18, 22; 2 Jn 7; 2 Thess 2:3–4, 8).

The coming of the Lord

Not only did Jesus describe future events, but he also, together with various writers, described the *manner* of his coming. Firstly, he will personally return to this earth, 'I will come back . . .' (John 14:3), 'Behold, I am coming soon!' (Rev 22:7), and 'the Lord himself will come down from heaven . . .' (1 Thess 4:16). Secondly, his return will be a literal as opposed to a 'spiritual' return. 'Jesus . . .will come back in the same way you have seen him go into heaven' (Acts 1:11). He went physically and literally, so we are encouraged to accept that he will return physically and literally.

Furthermore, it would be visibly and publicly, 'For as lightning that comes from the east is visible even in the west, so will be the coming of the Son of Man' (Matt 24:27); 'They will see the Son of Man coming on the clouds of the sky, with power and great glory' (Matt 24:30). John says, 'we shall see him as he is' (1 Jn 3:2; and see Rev 1:7).

Most of us probably do not need reminding that he also said that he would appear suddenly and dramatically. Lightning appears suddenly (Matt 24:27), the floods came suddenly upon the people in Noah's day (24:37), thieves arrive suddenly and unannounced (24:43), 'the Son of Man will come at an hour when you do not expect him' (Matt 24:44), 'in a flash, in the twinkling of an eye . . .' (1 Cor 15:52). 'So you also must be ready' (Matt 24:44).

But Scripture is equally emphatic that it will have geographic significance. It will be, as we have seen, to a particular *place* that Jesus returns, to Israel and the Mount of Olives (Acts 1:11; Zech 14:4). His return will be glorious (Matt 24:30; Rev 1:7; 1 Thess 4:17).

I had become familiar with these prophecies of the Lord Jesus. It was not difficult to see that we could well be in the last of the last days if these prophecies were taken as a yardstick to his coming, but I sensed there was much more that I had yet to grasp. I turned to the prophecies in the Hebrew Scriptures referring to the Messiah that are *yet* to be fulfilled. These were the passages from which Jesus himself was quoting, passages that speak of a future event. Thus:

The Messiah is to come with the clouds of heaven (Dan 7:13–14). This is confirmed in Matthew 24:30, 25:31, 26:64 and also in Mark 14:61–62; Acts 1:9–11; Revelation 1:7 cross referenced with Exodus 40:34–35.

The Messiah will come as judge (Mic 4:3). The New Covenant parallel: Jude 14–15; and the Messiah is to sit on the throne of David for ever (Isa 9:6–7), New Covenant parallel: Luke 1:32–33; Hebrews 1:8.

The Messiah is to reign over all the earth (Ps 72:8, 11). New Covenant parallel: (Philippians 2:9–11; Revelation 11:15, 19:11–16.

Logically it made sense to me was that if so much of Biblical prophecy had *already* been fulfilled in the life, death and resurrection of Jesus, then I could be confident that these future events will happen too.

There is a further set of prophecies concerning the Messiah that neither of these two approaches include. It might be summed up, If this prophecy then why not that? For example, if we consider Zechariah 9:9–10, in verse 9 we read, 'Rejoice greatly, O Daughter of Zion! Shout, Daughter of Jerusalem! See, your king comes to you, righteous and having salvation, gentle and riding on a donkey . . .'; The gospel writers see Jesus' triumphant entry into Jerusalem as fulfilling this. But what of verse 10, 'He (the same king as is spoken of in verse 9) will proclaim peace to the nations. His rule will extend from sea to sea and from the River to the ends of the earth.' If the first speaks of Jesus, then why not the second. Will we not see Jesus as King ruling over the earth?

In Isaiah chapter 9, Christians can accept Jesus as the 'Wonderful Counsellor, Mighty God, Everlasting Father, Prince of Peace' (9:6), but we struggle with verse 7: 'He will reign on David's throne and over his kingdom, establishing and upholding it with justice and righteousness from that time on and for ever.' If the first refers to Jesus, then why not the second?

To summarise future events, the Messiah will come one day on the clouds of heaven as Judge to sit on the throne of David for ever and reign over all the earth. Have we changed that prospect?

But this was exactly where my problems emerged. A throne (Isa 9:7) implies a king and a kingdom. Is it in heaven or is it on earth? To 'reign over all the earth'. Is that literal or spiritual? How do we know which is the right hermeneutic?

The usual answers revolve around the definition of the millennium (Rev 20:1–8) which speaks of Christ reigning for a thousand years. Is this literally, ie on earth, or spiritually?

I mentioned at the beginning of this book that there are three main views in the Christian Church concerning the coming of the Messiah and his millennial reign. Great saints of Church history have all held different opinions! Listed below are brief characteristics of each millennial view.

1. The Post-Millennial view.

The Second Coming of Christ will *follow* the millennium. The Kingdom of God is already here in the Church and will be extended through preaching the gospel.

Ultimately the Church will 'Christianise' the whole world and this will be the millennium. It will be followed by Armageddon and the return of Christ. Simultaneously there will be the resurrection and final judgment.

2. The A-Millennial view.

No physical millennial reign is expected on earth. The Second Coming will be preceded by apostasy and wickedness. The antichrist will appear and the Lord will defeat him at his Coming.

Simultaneously the resurrection and judgment will take place. The earth will be overwhelmed by fire, and a new heaven and new earth will be brought into being.

3. The Pre-Millennial view.

The millennial reign is a literal one thousand years.

Apostasy, tribulation and suffering will follow for, probably, seven years. During the last three and a half years, the antichrist will rule the world. Christ will return after the seven-year tribulation, and his return is triggered by the battle of Armageddon at which the antichrist is defeated. Satan is bound, and Jesus will reign for a thousand years.

After the thousand years, Satan is let loose again. He incites rebellion against Christ, is defeated and is cast into the lake of fire. At this time, the wicked are judged at the great white throne, and the eternal state begins.

There are variants of this view, especially *dispensationalism*. This school of thought, a variant of premillennialism, arose from the teaching of John Nelson Darby (1800–1882), founder of the Brethren movement. It is a theological approach to the Bible that divides history into ages or 'dispensations' ('a period of time during which man is tested in respect to his obedience to some specific revelation of the will of God'. *New Schofield Bible*, 1967. p 3, note 3). The seven dispensations are: innocence, conscience, human government, promise, law, the church (or grace) and the millennial kingdom. There are two returns, one is *for* his people (known as a secret 'rapture', from the Latin word *rapiemur*, meaning 'caught up'–1 Thess 4:17) and one return *with* his people.

For the dispensationalist, the future coming of the kingdom will not be one event, but a series of events: the secret rapture; followed by the Great Tribulation, the glorious appearing of Christ to Israel and the world, usually asserted to be seven years after the secret rapture, followed by the judgments or seals in Revelation, and the millennial reign. At the end of the thousand years will be the great satanical revolt, Christ's victory and the final judgment.

You can perhaps see how dry and dead these simple outlines are. It is only God's word that lives. But how do we arrive at a certain position? Indeed should we at all?

Israel is the key

I was now convinced that the key to interpreting the end times prophecies was how one handled Israel. If Israel is replaced by the Church, then the conclusions one draws from Biblical prophecy will be very different from those based on holding onto the covenant promises made to Israel and seeing the Church grafted into the natural olive tree that is the believing remnant of Israel. This believing remnant will be from both the house of Israel and from the house of Judah, as we have seen from Jeremiah 31:31–34.

I wonder if you have seen one of those drawings that are three dimensional if you focus into the picture rather than at the picture. Suddenly, from a meaningless backdrop, the subject literally lifts out of the page. In a similar way, taking 'Israel is

Israel is Israel!' and seeing Jesus as the one who will fulfil end times prophecies, the Hebrew Scriptures by now were speaking with such new clarity, that I dared to put together a picture that emerged of her restoration. In a similar way, my focus had been *at* the Scriptures concerning Israel but not *into* the Scriptures.

We explore that restoration in the next chapter.

Chapter 15

THE RESTORATION OF ISRAEL

We are working on the theory that God still has a plan for Israel. The reader may still be taking this as a hypothesis. We have seen the theory in Jesus' own ministry in relation to Israel. There appears to be no given point in the New Testament that declares 'God has finished with Israel.' The contrary would seem to be the case. You may wish to take this further thought as a hypothesis, that God's dealings with Israel unlock his revelation of future events, and put it to the test.

It is my observation that the Church today is confused about the great hope that lies before it. Like a plane in a wartime situation, showering metal strips to confuse approaching enemy missiles, Satan has delighted in confusing the Church as to the manner in which Jesus will return by encouraging every interpretation possible. Remember my plea, that God *has* revealed his plan and that it is found in the Bible. He desires that we be blessed by the hope of his return, and that, inspired by the Holy Spirit, the integrity of Scripture is that the Bible explains the Bible and that his purpose for Israel is central.

The *key* to understanding Biblical prophecy is the centrality of the lordship of Jesus Christ and the guidance of his Holy Spirit, the one who inspired the prophets. Peter writes,

'Above all, you must understand that no prophecy of Scripture came about by the prophet's own interpretation. For prophecy never had its origin in the will of man, but men spoke from God as they were carried along by the Holy Spirit' (2 Pet 1:20–21)

It is Scripture that declares his lordship and Scripture that points to the promises made of Israel's restoration as central to the manner of the Messiah's coming.

You will read some books and certainly hear some preachers link different prophetic Bible passages to events happening in Israel, the Middle East, or the world. May I leave the reader to do that? May I ask you as you read the different passages quoted and look up others and ask yourself, 'Has this been fulfilled, or am I seeing this being fulfilled today?' Other prophecies have *yet* to be fulfilled.

Firstly, there are three questions to consider:

If the curses, why not the blessings?

It is not too difficult to find passages in the Bible where the curses of God's sanctions within the Mosaic covenants are declared by God to Israel. Read any of the prophets and there is an abundance. Remember, we have seen that the Middle Eastern culture, unlike a Western framework, has the world-view that enables them to record the fierce anger of God and his deep and tender compassion and hold the paradox in tension.

If the curses are Israel's, then why not the blessings?

A few examples: In Isaiah 30:12 we read, 'Therefore, this is what the Holy One of Israel says: 'Because you have rejected this message, relied on oppression and depended on deceit . . .' There follows God's message of judgment (30:17), 'A thousand will flee at the threat of one; at the threat of five you will flee away, till you are left like a flagstaff on a mountain top, like a banner on a hill.' No doubt that speaks of Israel. Immediately we have a promise of restoration, 'Yet the Lord longs to be gracious to you; he rises to show you compassion . . . O people of Zion, who live in Jerusalem, you will weep no more. How gracious he will be when you cry for help! . . .' and then follows a message of comfort (30:18ff).

Interestingly the Authorised Version of the Oxford University Press Bible, given to Anna, my wife, at her confirmation, ascribes the message of judgment as being to Israel and the message of restoration as 'God's mercies towards His church'.

The same line of interpretation is seen in a number of places in that version. Isa 44:1 in the NIV heads the chapter, 'Israel the chosen' ('But now listen, O Jacob, my servant . . .'), whereas the Oxford AV has the heading, 'God comforteth the church with His promise'. Similar passages of restoration are attributed to the church whilst the passages of judgment are laid at Israel's door. It was this thinking that had reinforced much of my confusion. We have already considered that the church is *not* Israel, so if the judgment passages are rightfully Israel's then so are the passages of restoration!

If partial, then why not complete fulfilment?

We have seen that the New Testament writers saw prophecies fulfilled in the life of Jesus where we would have difficulty seeing their original setting as referring to the coming Messiah. The obvious example is, 'Out of Egypt I called my son', quoted by Matthew as speaking of Jesus coming back to the land of Israel from Egypt (Hosea 11:1, Matt 2:15). It really does not appear to speak of Jesus in its original setting in Hosea. So we will find that prophetic passages can have more than one fulfilment. The prophets spoke to their contemporary situation as well as speaking of things to come.

In Acts 15:16–18, James quotes Amos 9:11–12, 'In that day I will restore David's fallen tent . . . and all the nations [Gentiles] that bear my name'. The NIV heading is 'Israel's restoration'. If James sees verses 11 and 12 finding a partial fulfilment in the first Gentiles coming to faith in Acts, then why not a complete fulfilment at a future date in the other verses of restoration that are yet to happen?

With these additional principles and those summarised at the beginning of the chapter, what then are the signs of Israel's restoration?

A faithful remnant

If God has *not* finished with Israel, but is true to his covenant promises, then we shall continue to see a remnant within the Jewish community who believe that Jesus is the Messiah. At the time of writing, the Messianic movement amongst Jewish people discovering that Jesus is the Messiah is growing considerably and indicates that the remnant principle of God still stands. We must also see a turning to the Messiah among the house of *Israel*.

A hardening in part

As we consider the state of Israel and the Jewish people, Scripture states that we shall see a hardening of Jews, in part, to the gospel. As a nation they have rejected the Messiah, but individually part of the nation has received him. This does not need demonstrating. However, the sign that follows is 'until the full number of the Gentiles has come in' (Rom 11:25).

Preserving a peculiar people

The same word 'until' illustrates that God intends that the Jewish people remain a distinctive people. Jesus, speaking to his Jewish disciples about his Second Coming and the signs that would precede it, said, 'I tell you the truth, this generation [NIV footnote, or 'race'] will certainly not pass away until all these things have happened' (Luke 21:32).

As one writer put it, 'Pharaoh could not drown them, Nebuchadnezzar could not burn them, the lions could not eat them, the whale could not digest them and Haman could not hang them' (M R De Haan, '*The Jew and Palestine in Prophecy*', Zondervan, Michigan, 1950).

Enemies on your account

There are two polarities that are crucial in understanding the place of Israel in God's purposes. The first is that 'As far as the gospel is concerned, they are enemies on your account; but as far as election is concerned, they are loved on account of the patriarchs, for God's gifts and his call are irrevocable' (Rom 11:28–29).

Paul is talking to Gentiles (11:13), and reminds us that Israel are 'loved on account of the patriarchs' (28). *Of no other ethnic people does Scripture specifically say this*. For whose benefit are they loved? For *your* benefit and mine.

The gospel has come to the Gentiles, leaving Israel, in part, as enemies of the gospel. We have seen how this hardening in part led the synagogue to separate from the church. History has demonstrated all too clearly that the Jewish people have become enemies to the extent that Christian theology has lent support to pogroms and the Holocaust.

In the Bible we read of certainly three holocaust attempts: In Exodus 1, Pharaoh decreed that all Israelite baby boys had to be thrown into the Nile – a satanic attack to destroy the coming saviour of the nation Israel (Moses). In Esther 3:1ff, an attempt was made by Haman to destroy all Jews in the vast Persian kingdom of Xerxes, but it was thwarted by Mordecai and Queen Esther. In Matthew 2:16, King Herod ordered all boys of two and under in the Bethlehem region to be killed – again, in my view, a satanic attack to try and destroy the Saviour of the world who had already come.

Jewish people are today enemies on my account – as far as the gospel is concerned. It means that you and I *benefit* from their sin of unbelief. Paul has explained this earlier, 'because of their transgression, salvation has come to the *Gentiles*' (Rom 11:11). You and I have been freely included in God's plan of salvation. This salvation was given *first* to the Jews. We do not have to become Jewish. Paul goes on, 'their transgression means riches for the world' (11:12); 'their rejection is the reconciliation of the world' (11:15).

That is the light in which the Holocaust must be seen. It has enormous theological significance. With our finite minds, it is impossible to grasp the enormity of what happened. When I was small, my parents had a set of encyclopaedias. I was not an avid reader, but from the earliest age remember being haunted by pictures of the Holocaust. Even reading the cold-blooded statistics filled me with a numbness.

In Poland at Auschwitz, Belzec, Chelmo, Treblinka; in Germany at Bergen Belsen, Buchenwald, Dachau, Ravensbruck; in Czechoslovakia at Theresienstadt, these are some of the death camps where about six million men, women and children – mostly Jewish – were murdered. It has been reckoned that of the estimated European population of Jews in Europe in 1941, in Greece, of 67,000 Jewish people 65,000 lost their lives; in Bulgaria, of 48,000 alive prior to the Holocaust, 40,000 died; in Romania, 750,000 of a Jewish population of one million were exterminated; in Yugoslavia 60,000 died of a population of 70,000 in 1941; from Russia, 750,000 went to the gas chambers out of 2.5 million Jews alive in 1941; in Latvia, of 100,000 Jews alive in 1941, 70,000 lost their lives; and in Lithuania, 104,000 died out of 140,000 alive in 1941.

Could any figures be worse than these? But in Poland, a staggering 2,600,000 Jews out of a population estimated at 3 million in 1941 went to the death camps, never to return. From Czechoslovakia, 277,000 perished out of a Jewish population in 1941 of 281,000; in Austria, 65,000 were killed of 70,000

Jews alive in 1941; in Germany itself, 180,000 Jews died out of a population of 250,000; from the Netherlands, 106,000 perished out of 140,000 Jews living there in 1941; from Belgium, 28,000 perished out of 85,000 Jews living there before the Holocaust; and from France, of 300,000 Jews alive in 1941, 83,000 died in the Holocaust.

Of the total of approximately six million who were killed, 1.5 million were children and many were believers in the Messiah. If that were averaged over those five years, it would mean that about 3,300 were systematically exterminated each day. Imagine your church, or your school assembly, or a hall that you know well. Imagine it full. How many people would it hold? How many times a day would you have to fill that building to make up a total of 3,300? Picture that happening, not just for one day, or a week, or a month, but *every day for five years*. Imagine you are in the hall or church yourself. It would mean your row, the row in front. The person next to you. *Jesus himself* would have been gassed and cremated. Such is the enormity of the Holocaust. 'Enemies' Paul says, 'on *your* account' (Rom 11:28). Could he ever have conceived such horror?

It took the Holocaust for the world to recognise the need of the Jewish people for their land and it took the Holocaust to persuade many Jews that they *had* to have a land in order to survive.

Such is the ferocity of Satan's opposition to the gospel that we too might have been the objects of persecution. I might have been in that queue. You might have. We might never have heard of the love of God shown in Jesus Christ.

I was challenged to consider that God's love, the love that has been 'poured . . . into hearts by the Holy Spirit, whom he has given us', as Paul says in Rom 5:5, is the same love that he has for the Jewish people. 'Loved on account of the patriarchs.' If God had poured his love into my heart and loves the Jewish people because of the patriarchs, then I too had to learn to love the people whom he loves.

Chapter 16

SIGNS OF A RETURN

The NIV has chapter divisions and headings at various places in the text and the heading, 'Restoration of Israel' appears frequently. I could never appreciate the passages because I did not see how they could be applied to me or my church situation. But they fitted with Israel! I would ask that you check Israel's circumstances and Scripture as this chapter unfolds.

A return that is a sovereign work of God

The land, or the *Place* as we have been calling it, has been sworn on oath by God to be the inheritance of Israel. There are over 100 such references to this in the Old Testament. We have seen that the covenant promises are everlasting and so too is the promise of the land to Israel (Gen 13:15, 17:8, 48:4, Ex 32:13, 1 Chron 16:15–18, 28:8, 2 Chron 20:7, Ps 37:29, Isa 60:21, Jer 7:7, 25:5).

In sovereign manner, God promises to bring them back to the land. All the prophets speak of the restoration of Israel. If we take the chapters from Jeremiah where the New Covenant is promised, there too is the promised restoration of the land, 'See, I will bring them from the land of the north and gather them from the ends of the earth' (Jer 31:8 and also 10, 16, 23).

But this return prophesied in Jeremiah primarily speaks of the return from Babylon where he is prophesying that the people of Judah will go. So it had to be Zechariah who returned to Israel *after* the exile that would convince me of another return. Sure enough, there it was. 'This is what the Lord Almighty says, "I will save my people from the countries of the east and the west. I will bring them back to live in Jerusalem; . . . and I will be faithful and righteous to them as their God"' (Zech 8:7–8; 10:8,10).

At least four groups will almost certainly say a definite 'No!' to a physical return to the land of Israel. The first, those who say the Church has replaced Israel. The second, those orthodox Jewish people who believe in the coming Messiah, but see *him* as the one who leads them back to the land. The third and fourth groups, those who politically or on grounds of religion believe such a return must be fought tooth and nail.

A return in unbelief

It was in my understanding of the secular state of Israel that many of my problems were rooted, until I understood that the people of Israel would return, largely in unbelief. In Ezekiel 20:30ff, a passage headed in the NIV, 'Judgment and restoration', the Sovereign Lord says, 'I will bring you from the nations and gather you from the countries where you have been scattered (v34)' . . . 'and I will show myself holy among you in the sight of the nations. *Then* you will know that I am the Lord' (vv41–42). First the physical restoration, *then* the spiritual restoration.

Clearly this spiritual restoration is something that has *yet* to happen. God *is* drawing his people back to the land, but (at the time of writing) he has not yet shown himself holy among Israel in the sight of the nations, and Israel as a nation, whether in the land or scattered in the Diaspora, does not yet know that Jesus the Messiah is the Lord.

In his parallel passage to Jeremiah's prophecy concerning the New Covenant in Ezekiel 36, the order of restoration is spelt out again,

'For I will take you out of the nations; I will gather you from all the countries and bring you back into your own land. I will sprinkle clean water on you . . . I will cleanse you from all your impurities . . .' (Ezek 36:24, 25).

The return comes first, *then* the receiving of forgiveness. *First* the physical restoration, *then* the spiritual restoration.

In the vision of the valley of the dry bones (37:1–14), physical life comes into the bones first, and spiritual life only comes afterwards. Furthermore, this prophecy concerns the coming together of the both the house of Israel and the house of Judah, as intimated in previous chapters of this book.

A return where injustices will still be seen

Justice is a recurring theme in the prophets. Old Testament prophets did not merely foretell, but forthtell God's word to contemporary society. There is perhaps no nation on earth where the question of justice is not scrutinised by the world as the degree to which it is in Israel. It is as though God uses the world's media to spotlight issues that are perceived as unjust.

The return in unbelief (Jer 30:3,10; 31:8,10,16,17,23 *et al*) precedes Jeremiah 31:31–34 foretelling restoration to the Lord. This means that we are not to be expected to see all the circumstances of the return as God's perfect plan. Israel comes back to the land in unbelief and in unbelief will conduct their affairs, *until* God's sovereign circumstances that bring his covenanted people to know him and when his law will be in their hearts and minds.

This does not mean that we automatically side with Israel when any injustice is caused. The alien has rights and we can remind Israel of this. Palestinians and Arabs who have made Israel their home come under that Biblical, and somewhat unhelpful word 'alien'. 'When an alien lives with you in your land, do not ill-treat him. The alien living with you must be treated as one of your native-born. Love him as yourself, for you were aliens in Egypt' (Lev 19:33, 34). The question of aliens living in the land was not dismissed lightly by the Lord (also Ex 22:21), 'You are to have same law for the alien and the native-born' (Lev 24:22), 'The Lord watches over the alien . . .' (Ps 146:9). Israel might be inheritors of the land, but God took very seriously the issue of justice and the rights of the alien. If the return is in unbelief, then there will inevitably be conflict with the alien and that means the Palestinians and Arabs clashing over their own particular claims to the land.

Before we are too quick to judge, we could ask ourselves how we treat aliens in our own nation. Anti-Semitism can appear in the disguise of judging Israel by a standard that we ourselves would not even match.

A return a second time

We have seen in Zechariah 8:7–8, *after* the return from Babylon, that a further return to the land was promised. It made sense of Isaiah 11:11–12, 'In that day the Lord will reach out his hand *a second time* to reclaim the remnant that is left of his people from Assyria . . .'.

A return not just from Babylon

Isaiah 11:11–12 continues,

> In that day the Lord will reach out his hand *a second time* to reclaim the remnant that is left of his people from Assyria, from Lower Egypt, from Upper Egypt, from Cush, from Elam, from Babylonia, from Hamath and from the islands of the sea . . . he will assemble the scattered people of Judah from the four quarters of the earth.

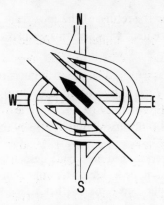

Consider the number of nations from which Israel has received returning Jews! (See also Jer 24:6; Ezek 36:8–10, 24; Amos 9:14, 15.)

The Babylonian return was hardly from the north, south, east and west as Isaiah prophesies (Isa 43:5–6)!

A return not just in a small number

The return from the Babylonian exile records that around 50,000 returned, mainly from the house of Judah, whereas Jeremiah records,

> 'So then, the days are coming', declares the Lord, 'when people will no longer say, "As surely as the Lord lives, who brought the Israelites up out of Egypt", but they will say, "As surely as the Lord lives, who brought the descendants of Israel up out of the land of the north and out of all the countries where he had banished them"' (Jer 23:7–8).

We have seen that the Exodus from Egypt is *the* event that reminded Israel of God's sovereign hand in the forming of the nation. Now there is to be a day when a return of Jews to the land will eclipse even that mighty escape. As you read these verses concerning the return of the Jews from all over the world, may I ask the reader whether this return is still continuing today.

A return to the land that will seem too small for them

To Israel, the prophet Isaiah addresses the words,

'Though you were ruined and made desolate and your land laid waste, now you will be too small for your people . . . The children born during your bereavement [that refers to the time of the people's exile from the land] will yet say in your hearing, "This place is too small for us; give us more space to live in"' (Isa 49:19–20).

Is that an issue today in the land of Israel as you read these words of Isaiah?

A return as one kingdom, not two

Following those well-known words of Ezekiel in the vision of the valley of the dry bones that refer to the 'whole house of Israel' (37:11) (not the Church, as I had first believed – although of some churches, the dry bones may seem very apt!), the Lord promises restoration: 'I will bring you back to the land of Israel. *Then* you, my people, will know that I am the Lord' (37:12–13). First, the physical restoration, then the spiritual restoration.

The promise continues, 'I will make them *one* nation in the land, on the mountains of Israel' (Ezek 37:22). That means that the house of Israel and the house of Judah reunite.

A return 'after many generations'

Speaking of the return to the land, Isaiah says, 'They will rebuild the ancient ruins and restore the places long devastated;

they will renew the ruined cities that have been devastated for generations' (Isa 61:4). The exile to Babylon was for a period of seventy years (Jer 25:11, 29:10, Dan 9:2). That is just less than two generations. That exile was within the life span of one person, whereas the passage in Isaiah speaks of a long devastation of many generations (implied). Go to the Jewish Quarter in Jerusalem and see how they have repaired the devastation after many generations.

A return in circumstances of great suffering

'See, I will bring them from the land of the north and gather them from the ends of the earth. Among them will be the blind and the lame, expectant mothers and women in labour; a great throng will return. They will come weeping, they will pray as I bring them back' (Jer 31:8–9).

The return from Babylon was not difficult. It came with a royal edict from King Artaxerxes (Neh 1:5–8; 2:6), whereas the return from all the lands where God scattered his people, especially the lands of the north, was a return that included the devastating grief of the Holocaust. (See also Jer 31:15–17, 16:14–16, 30:1–7).

A return where 'foreigners will work your fields'

'Aliens will shepherd your flocks; foreigners will work your fields and vineyards' (Isa 61:5). This was not so in Ezra's and Nehemiah's day after the first return from exile, for they had to exclude foreigners from having any part in the work. When Nehemiah was ridiculed by Sanballat the Horonite, Tobiah the Ammonite and Geshem the Arab following his announcement of rebuilding the walls of Jerusalem, he records, 'I answered them by saying, "The God of heaven will give us success . . . but as for you, you have no share in Jerusalem or any claim or historic right to it"' (Neh 2:20).

A return when Christians will proclaim the coming King

There is an interesting prophecy in Isaiah (62:11–12) that indicates that God will call those who know him as Saviour to 'say to the Daughter of Zion, "See, your Saviour comes! See, his reward is with him . . ."' Then Isaiah continues, 'They [speaking of those from the ends of the earth] will be called the Holy People, the Redeemed of the Lord; and you [the Daughter of Zion] will be called Sought After, the City No Longer Deserted'.

A return never to be rejected again as a nation

'This is what the Lord says, he who appoints the sun to shine by day, who decrees the moon and stars to shine by night, who stirs up the sea so that its waves roar – the Lord Almighty is his name: "*Only* if these decrees vanish from my sight", declares the Lord, "will the descendants of Israel ever cease to be a nation before me"' (Jer 31:35–36). Somehow that could not be clearer. I am persuaded that were the present state of Israel to be defeated and driven from the land, yet God is bound by his covenant faithfulness to restore his people. I am actually persuaded that this *is* the return promised in Scripture, with all the inherent difficulties and questions that it raises.

A return never to be scattered again

Not only is Israel never to cease as a nation, but never to be scattered again. Prophesying to the land, Ezekiel speaks God's word, 'I will cause people, my people Israel, to walk upon you . . . and you will be their inheritance; you will never again deprive them of their children' (Ezek 36:12).

Ezekiel cannot be prophesying the return from Babylon, because the Jews were exiled again in AD 70 and not to return in significant numbers for nearly 2,000 years.

Amos concludes his book under the NIV heading, 'Israel's restoration', with these words, 'I will bring back my exiled people Israel . . . I will plant Israel in their own land, *never again* to be uprooted from the land I have given them' (Amos 9:14–15). Jeremiah adds, 'The city [Jerusalem] will never again be uprooted or demolished' (Jer 31:40).

During the Gulf War in 1991, America and the allies put great pressure on Israel not to counter Saddam Hussein's scud missile attacks. Who was behind Israel's protection?

How incredible to read, soon after Operation Desert Storm had ended so abruptly, that 40 scuds had been fired on Israel, one had been blown off course and 39 had landed (almost like 40 lashes less one). Amazingly, there had been only one fatality, with story after story of miraculous escapes. Was there significance in the abrupt ending of the hostilities – with so much that seemed unresolved, that the war had, as one press report stated, lasted 40 days and 40 nights – on the very day of the Feast of Purim, when Jewish people celebrate the rescue of the Jews in Babylon from Haman's plot to have them all destroyed, the very land from which these attacks were coming and were similarly defeated?

Is God not sovereign and is his word not sure?

'"The grass withers and the flowers fall, but the word of God stands for ever." You who bring good tidings to Zion . . . to Jerusalem, lift up your voice with a shout . . . say to the towns of Judah, "Here is your God!" See, the Sovereign Lord comes with power . . . He tends his flock like a shepherd: He gathers the lambs in his arms and carries them close to his heart; he gently leads those that have young' (Isa 40:8–11).

A return for his holy name's sake

Ezekiel prophesies,

'This is what the Sovereign Lord says: "it is not for your sake, O house of Israel, that I am going to do these things, but for the sake of my holy name which you have profaned among the nations where you have gone' . . . "I want you to know that I am not doing this for your sake, declares the Sovereign Lord" (Ezek 36:22–32).

Here, the prophet is saying that the name of the Lord, that is Jesus Christ, is profaned among the nations. His name has become a swear word and blasphemy is common place. God is saying that he is going to act for his holy name's sake.

A return for a purpose

Ezekiel continues in the passage quoted above, 'I will show the holiness of my great name . . . '*Then* the nations will know that I am the Lord, declares the Sovereign Lord, when I show myself holy through you before their eyes' (Ez 36:23). Here is a remarkable thing. God is bringing Israel back to the land and will reveal himself holy to them and among them in such a way that the nations will know that the Sovereign Lord is God.

The return is a physical outworking of the spiritual return of Israel to the Lord. *First* the physical return, *then* the spiritual return to their Messiah.

If the Lord is to bless the nations through the return of the Jews to the Messiah, then he must first bless the Jews with salvation *before* they are to bless us Gentiles. 'They will be my people, and I will be their God' (Jer 32:38).

A return with signs that will be observable

We have seen that Jesus gave a significant number of signs that are going to be clearly observable leading up to his return. Having said that he had come to fulfil the Prophets (Matt 5:17), then his teaching in Matthew 24 and Luke 21 can be seen as bringing into sharper focus the prophecies in the Hebrew Scriptures concerning the circumstances of his return.

Just as the prophets encourage us to see a literal, physical restoration of Israel followed by a spiritual restoration of the nation to the Messiah, so the prophets encourage us to look for a physical return of the Messiah. Jesus does too, and he presents the circumstances leading to his return from a Jerusalem-centred perspective: 'standing in the holy place' (Matt 24:15), 'let those who are in Judea' (16), and 'out in the desert' (26).

A return of Jerusalem to Jewish rule

Jesus had prophesied, 'When you see Jerusalem being surrounded by armies, you will know that its desolation is near . . .' (Luke 21:20). We have seen that this reference gave advance warning to the Messianic believers to flee during the siege of Jerusalem under Titus in AD 70. Four verses later, he says, 'Jerusalem will be trampled on by the Gentiles until the times of the Gentiles are fulfilled' (21:24), and, similarly, we have seen this fulfilled and will, no doubt, continue to see the legitimacy of Israel's rule over the city hotly contested.

A return in time of great trouble

Jesus speaks of a 'distress unequalled from the beginning of the world until now – and never to be equalled again' (Matt 24:21, and see v29). He is recalling the words of the prophet Daniel (12:1) and observes, 'If those days had not been cut short, no-one would survive, but for the sake of the elect those days will be shortened' (Matt 24:22).

Jeremiah indicates that in the context of the return to the land there would be a terrible time, 'How awful that day will be! None will be like it. It will be a time of trouble for Jacob, but he will be saved out of it' (Jer 30:7).

A peace when there is no peace

Both Jeremiah and Ezekiel prophesy 'Peace, peace . . . when there is no peace' (Jer 6:14, 8:11; Ezek 13:10). True peace is only found in the Prince of Peace (Isa 9:6). A day seems to be foretold when Israel will feel secure and unsuspecting, and will be invaded (Ezek 38:11ff).

Jerusalem surrounded by an all nations army

Zechariah speaks of a further siege of Jerusalem, 'On that day, when all the nations of the earth are gathered against her' (Zech 12:3) and that this is God's doing, 'I will gather all the nations to Jerusalem to fight against it' (14:2). It is worth noting that the Gulf War in 1991 was the first time that such a significant all nations army was employed. Consider affairs in the Middle East today. Could it be that even as you read this book, an alliance of nations, with the endorsement of the United Nations, could be mobilised as a solution to the region's problems and especially Israel's actions as perceived by world opinion? Scripture prophesies that it will happen. Consider the consequences for the nations that take part (Zech 12:3b–6, and 9 especially, 14:1–3, 12–15).

As an aside, the frequently employed phrase 'On that day' in the prophets had always caused me difficulties. I had tried in vain to squeeze all that happens 'on that day' into a 24-hour time period and the result is – nonsense! I am helped to believe that it rather refers to the period of time that God is publicly and visibly acting in Israel and the nations in various sovereign ways. If that is right, then God is at work before the very eyes of the world.

Jerusalem, a 'cup of reeling'

Piecing together the chronology of events is not easy, but I began to see that Zechariah, having prophesied a return to the land, then records the word of the Lord concerning Israel. 'I am going to make Jerusalem a cup that sends all surrounding peoples reeling' (12:2). It is as though nations that attempt to interfere with God's plans for that city become disorientated.

It is as though we shall continue to see different world leaders attempting to find solutions to the question of Jerusalem and their efforts will lead to their failing to see whose city it is anyway! Jeremiah foretold, 'At that time they will call Jerusalem The Throne of the Lord, and all nations will gather in Jerusalem to honour the name of the Lord' (3:17). Thus Zechariah prophesies, 'All who try to move it [Jerusalem] will injure themselves' (Zech 12:3). We could take that statement as a hypothesis and test it. Is it true that those who have attempted to exert pressure over the status of Jerusalem since 1948 have indeed injured themselves?

The rise of the antichrist

'Concerning the coming of our Lord Jesus Christ . . . Don't let anyone deceive you in any way, for that day will not come until the rebellion occurs and the man of lawlessness is revealed, the man doomed to destruction' (2 Thess 2:1,3). How crucial for the Church to be ready for such a world ruler! If we 'spiritu-alise' everything, then we will not be looking in the contemporary world for such a person to emerge onto the world scene. How then could we warn the world? The very group in the West that should be warning the world of such a terrible situation is itself largely agnostic on the subject!

Third temple, Gog and Magog and the rapture

I am deliberately leaving these three issues out of this overview of forthcoming events for obvious reasons. My sincere belief is that we can so easily follow this or that person's view, or buy an 'off-the-peg end times scenario' and not have a deep inner Biblical and peaceful conviction about aspects of the elements that make up that scenario. My apologies to those who have read all this way only to find that these are now omitted! If salvation history can be seen as a 16mm film reel, then God has given us clues as to which future scenes probably follow what. Over to you!

The return of Israel to the Messiah

In the context of the armies surrounding Jerusalem in Zechariah 12, the prophet writes,

'I will pour out on the house of David and the inhabitants of Jerusalem a spirit of grace and supplication. They will look on me, the one they have pierced, and they will mourn for him as one mourns for an only child, and grieve bitterly for him as one grieves for a firstborn son' (12:10).

We have considered the 'this is that' principle, drawn from the day of Pentecost, where Peter demonstrates that Acts 2:17–21 fulfils Joel 2:28–32. Similarly in Paul's statement, 'All Israel will be saved' (Rom 11:26) and 'this is my covenant . . . when I take away their sins' (Rom 11:27) and 'how much greater riches will their fulness bring!' (Rom 11:12). *This* passage in Zechariah is part of *that* explanation in Paul.

The year of the Lord's favour

We see in Isaiah 61:1–2 words that Jesus read out in the synagogue at Nazareth,

'The Spirit of the Lord is on me, because he has anointed me to preach good news to the poor. He has sent me to proclaim freedom for the prisoners and recovery of sight for the blind, to release the oppressed, to proclaim the year of the Lord's favour' (Lk 4:18, 19).

He stops at that point. But Isaiah continues with a message of comfort to Zion that indicates that God will honour his jubilee of favour. 'Instead of their shame my people will receive a double portion, and instead of disgrace they will rejoice in their inheritance; and so they will inherit a double portion in their land, and everlasting joy will be theirs' (Isa 61:7). Doubly punished as God's son (Ex 4:22), Israel will one day be doubly blessed.

Most of us will remember the incredible rapidity with which the former Soviet Union collapsed and how the Berlin Wall fell. Few were bold enough to predict it. The issue of praying for and calling on the Soviet authorities to let Jewish people out of Russia had gone on for years and then, suddenly, the Wall was breached and those who wanted to leave now had the chance. What struck me, as I read the report in the *Jewish Chronicle* was that the Wall fell within days of the Jewish Jubilee year of 5750. Had not God's word been, 'I will say to the north, "Give them up"' (Isa 43:6)? Did not Jesus speak much about the timing of all that he did ('My time has not yet come' – Jn 2:4, and, 'Father, the time has come' – Jn 17:1 et al)? Had the Father not set times and dates by 'his own authority' (Acts 1:7)? Was it not with precision that he had, in the Messiah, fulfilled the festivals, Passover and Pentecost? This was staggering if it were true.

I had distanced myself from those into Biblical numerology, but this was as though God had challenged my understanding of his ability, within modern history, to act with the sovereignty that he had in Bible history. Had not Britain recognised answer to prayer in the circumstances that enabled the evacuation of Dunkirk during the war? Then why not God's word to his people behind the Iron Curtain? It was as though here was Biblical prophecy being fulfilled under the very noses of the world's media and yet they could not see it. A Jubilee gesture by the God of Abraham.

Was it coincidence that the call for a Jewish homeland in the Basle Declaration of 1897 was echoed 50 years later by the ratification of the homeland by the United Nations in November 1947? Was there any connection between General Allenby's victory in Palestine in December 1917 (when he walked into the city of Jerusalem, as a devout Bible-believing Christian, his head bared in recognition that this event had Biblical significance) and, 50 years later, in 1967, when Jerusalem was once again in Jewish hands? Jesus' word had been, 'Jerusalem will be trampled on by the Gentiles until the times of the Gentiles are fulfilled' (Lk 21:24). God is a God of timing and he still takes his Jubilee promises seriously.

Of course there is no way to prove any of these thoughts, perhaps in the same way that we may struggle to prove answers to prayer to an unbeliever.

The return of the Messiah

Has God finished with Israel? If the Biblical accounts of the return of the Lord Jesus Christ are to be treated seriously, even if it is difficult to piece everything together, then Israel is still central to his coming.

In the context of Jerusalem being attacked by the nations and Israel seeing him whom they crucified, Zechariah speaks of the Lord returning to the Mount of Olives (Zech 14:4). Is that not exactly where the angels said he would return at his ascension from the Mount of Olives? 'Men of Galilee . . . This same Jesus, who has been taken from you into heaven, will come back in the same way you have seen him go into heaven' (Acts 1:11). Again, we could argue, this in Acts is that prophesied in Zechariah.

Israel is the context of his return. Little wonder that there will always be satanic attempts to prevent his return. First the return of the Jews back to the land, largely in unbelief. And was the Holocaust, indeed Hitler's strategy to seize control of Palestine, was indeed a satanic attempt to thwart the return? Why should that be? It is because *without the return of the people to the land, there can be no return of the Lord*. If the Church cannot see what is happening in the events of Israel and the whole Middle East, then how can the world?

New heavens and a new earth

'Behold, I will create new heavens and a new earth. The former things will not be remembered, nor will they come to mind. But be glad and rejoice for ever in what I will create, for I will create Jerusalem to be a delight and its people a joy. I will rejoice over Jerusalem and take delight in my people; the sound of weeping and of crying will be heard in it no more' (Isa 65:17–19).

At last heaven has arrived! Surely here is the everlasting bliss? Still we find that the context is Jerusalem, but problems have appeared, for Isaiah continues,

'Never again will there be in it an infant who lives but a few days, or an old man who does not live out his years; he who dies at a hundred will be thought a mere youth; he who fails to reach a hundred will be considered accursed'(20).

There is no death in heaven (Rev 21:4). The prophet Isaiah adds, 'They will build houses and dwell in them; they will plant vineyards and eat their fruit' (Isa 65:21). Jesus told us that 'In my Father's house are many rooms . . . I am going there to prepare a place for you' (Jn 14:2). How come in the 'new heavens and a new earth' of Isaiah 65, there are people building houses and planting vineyards?

The problem arises if the Church has taken to itself all the promises that concern Israel for this and many, many other such promises which simply do not fit with the Church. However, if the Lord is coming back to reign as King, then we see here an earthly period of his rule and reign.

'As the new heavens and the new earth that I make will endure before me', declares the Lord, 'so will your name and descendants endure' (Isa 66:22). Read on to see if Isaiah is talking about heaven! We have already seen that 'new' in Hebrew (chadash) means 'renew'. Our sad and war-torn world is to be renewed!

Jesus is the key

If we are reading this as committed believers in Jesus as Messiah, then we would agree that he is the key to understanding world events and the coming age, for 'at the name of Jesus every knee should bow, in heaven and on earth and under the earth, and every tongue confess that Jesus Christ is Lord, to the glory of God the Father' (Phil 2:10–11).

If I could propose an analogy, I submit that if Jesus holds the key to future events, then he has chosen Israel to be a number of the levers of the key without which you cannot turn the flick bolts in the lock of the door. He promised Abraham a *People*, a *Place*, for a *Purpose* and that it would be in *Perpetuity*. I wonder if those four promises act like four of the levers of the key and he acts within history using these four levers among others, for he says, 'I am coming soon' (Rev 22:20).

You will not be surprised

Paul wrote, 'you, brothers, are not in darkness so that this day should surprise you like a thief' (1 Thess 5:4). Jesus warned us that he would come like a thief in the night (Lk 12:39–40), but here Paul is saying that this day should not surprise us. History is so littered with accounts of those who have thought that the end of the world is coming on such and such a date that we have become extremely wary of any suggestion that we can have any certainty about the circumstances of his return. It is as though we have not only thrown the baby out with the bathwater, but

we have thrown the bath out as well! Paul seems to say otherwise.

How could it be that we should not be surprised? I believe
that the answer lies in Jesus' words, 'Keep watch . . .' (Matt
24:42–44). Like the householder who is warned that there will
be a break in, we are to make precautions, listen and watch for
his coming. It is events that Jesus has described in his discourse
on the signs of the end of the age (as the NIV heads Matthew
24), and it is events for which we must look.

Is there any area of our spiritual lives, as those who follow
Jesus the Messiah and accept him as Lord, in which we do not
have to grow? It makes sense then, that in the area of watching
(as he commanded), we will need to grow in our understanding
of what to watch out for and how to discern events that will
enable us, as Paul says, not to be in darkness so that the day
should surprise us like a thief.

If the thesis is correct, and I have to leave it with the reader
to test this out, then, if God has not finished with Israel, we will
continue to see Israel, ie the circumstances concerning the
Jewish people, the land of Israel itself, and the wider question
of the house of Israel, as levers of the key that unlocks the door
to the Lord's return. We will grow in our understanding as we
look in that direction for the following reasons:

Israel was the focus of Jesus' ministry and a priority of the
early Church. Paul affirms the future of Israel and the prophets speak of her restoration. All that is, however, Biblical, and
the Bible closes at the end of the first century. What of history
since? Can we grow in our understanding of world events and
see God's hand in the direction that circumstances and events
have taken and are taking? If we can, then we will be more
equipped to watch and not be surprised.

Israel's history teaches us three principles of understanding
world history, among many.

Firstly, you reap what you sow (Gal 6:7). Just as a person
reaps what he sows, either in sinful wrongdoing or in doing

good, so the nation Israel did too. David's adultery is cited as the cause of so much of Israel's resulting disaster (2 Sam 12:10–12). So in history, we will see events that are the reaping of things sown in the years gone by. God's word stands and we will grow as we ask the question, What was sown in the past that has reaped this world event or that?

Secondly, a nation gets the leaders it deserves. Israel's Biblical history demonstrates the tragedy of corrupt leadership and blessing of wise leadership. As we look at world events we too will see that principle.

But there is a third area in which we can grow in discernment. We have seen the promises made to Abraham repeated in the four levers of the key to the coming of the Lord: a *People*, a *Place*, for a *Purpose* in *Perpetuity*. Within that set of promises were the simple words, 'I will bless those who bless you, and whoever curses you I will curse' (Gen 12:3).

Chapter 17

I WILL BLESS THOSE WHO BLESS YOU

We are considering how we might discern God's sovereign activity amongst the nations as he turns the key of his Coming. Just as keys have levers to turn the lock in a door, so there are levers in this key.

We have noted God's promises to Abraham, but we have not looked more closely at his words 'I will bless those who bless you, and whoever curses you I will curse' (Gen 12:3).

My line of enquiry here is that if this promise could be seen to be true, both in the Bible and in history, then our discernment of God's activity in our time would grow.

Firstly, was God true to this promise in the Scriptures? As if to make an immediate point to Abraham, the Lord inflicts serious disease on Pharaoh for the way he (apparently unwittingly) took Sarai into his palace (Gen 12:17). Abimalech suffered in Genesis 20 and was blessed as he vindicated Abraham (20:17,18). Certainly Egypt experienced blessing as it 'blessed' Joseph and his family as they came down in the famine, and experienced curses on the land through its later cruelty to the children of Israel.

The account of Balaam in Numbers 22 further illustrates God's faithfulness to his word of promise. Balaam was approached by Balak, king of Moab, to put a curse on the

173

Israelites, 'For I know that those you bless are blessed, and those you curse are cursed' (22:6b), the very promise we consider here.

Later, in God's dealings with Israel, this time in his anger, he dispersed them to Babylon. It is Babylon that is chastened for her dealings with Israel. They were called to discipline the nation but they were judged for the way they did so, as Jeremiah records, '"Before your eyes I will repay Babylon and all who live in Babylonia for all the wrong they have done in Zion," declares the Lord' (Jer 51:24).

The question I want to ask is, 'Does this promise to Abraham still stand today? Does God still bless those who bless Abraham and his descendants or should we see this only as a spiritual blessing?' If God has finished with Israel, then to pursue this would be futile, but supposing he has not?

I was in Israel some years ago and, on the recommendation of a friend, went with my wife and family to The Museum of the Diaspora on the campus at Tel Aviv University. It proved to be a seminal experience.

The Museum was really a multi-media presentation of the entire 4,000 year history of Israel and the Jewish people, with no expense spared. One could easily spend a day there. I do not think that it is the intention of those behind the presentation, but I came away with an overwhelming sense that I had walked down the centre of history. It was as though world history bowed to the migration, the blessing or the cursing of Israel and this tiny ethnic group of people. As one progressed through the different time periods of history, with maps and pictures and displays, it was evident that nations rose and fell according to the relationship that they had with this small but chosen people.

I am raising the question as to how we can grow in our discernment of God's hand in the warp and woof of history's rich tapestry, how we can be watchful and not be surprised by the Day that is coming. I write this part of my testimony, open to being considered somewhat foolish as I am no historian, and the hypothesis could be killed stone dead by a thousand qualifications (it smacks of Zionism, it lacks real scholarship, and so on). I offer it only as a hypothesis that the reader may wish to test or merely note. In one sense, I am not pleading that what I now write is right! What I *am* pleading is that we learn to uphold Scripture and see that Jesus, the Messiah and coming King, commands us to watch. How else is he able to see that we are not surprised by the events if we do not start somewhere and discern his hand in history?

I know that history is *his* story, and when one stops to think about it, one key strand in his story is about a *People* to whom he promised a *Place* and a *Purpose*, a purpose to bless all peoples with the gospel, and that these promises would be in *Perpetuity*. It is into these promises that he has grafted Gentiles who believe and trust that Jesus Christ is Lord. We do not inherit the land, but we are members of the commonwealth of Israel that does inherit this promise.

Seeing the multi-media presentation in Tel Aviv, I found myself stumbling upon what I began to see were possible examples of this rising and falling of nations (and individuals) in history, according to their relationship with Jewish people or Israel. Could it be that this promise of God to bless those who bless the Hebrew people is similarly one of the little levers on the key that unlocks something of the mysteries of history's otherwise inexplicable randomness?

If Jesus Christ has 'all authority in heaven and on earth' (Matt 28:18), then he is sovereign in history and in the affairs of men. If this particular promise of blessing is still a promise that God honours, then what a staggering truth that nations need to hear! Historians are unlikely to attempt writing from a Biblical perspective such as this, and foreign affairs have national self-interest at heart, so what I write here will find little support from historians and politicians. I now enter the lions' den!

Is it coincidence that once Constantine embarked on his anti-Semitic laws as Emperor and persecuted the Jews that, in AD

364, the Empire was split in two? Is it chance that, as Jews were hounded from one country to another from then on, we entered the Dark Ages?

Could it be coincidence that Richard the Lionheart, who led the Third Crusade to the Holy Land in 1190–1, exacting tribute from the Jews to fund the crusade and involved in the massacre of thousands of Jews, both in Europe and in Jerusalem, was himself imprisoned by Leopold of Austria on his return to England and a ransom of 150,000 marks was demanded to release him, twice England's estimated gross national product?

Is it coincidence that Spain's demise as a world power dates from 1492, the year 300,000 Spanish Jewry were expelled? Is there a connection that exactly 500 years later, when the Declaration of Expulsion was finally repealed, Spain experienced the blessing of the harvest of those finding the Lord Jesus at Expo '92 in Seville, an exhibition at which so many came to faith in Jesus Christ through the Pavilion, 'Hall of Promise', fruit that had never been seen in Spain on that scale before?

Does this explain why Martin Luther died in the very week that he preached his most vitriolic sermon against the Jews, part of which I have quoted in a previous chapter, a sermon that Hitler would later wave as the thinking of the Church and therefore, in his eyes, support for his 'final solution'?

Might this promise of God explain why Germany was so crushed through World War II as a result of the horrors of Holocaust (or Shoah, as Jewish people now call it) and divided in two for nearly half a century by the Iron Curtain, experiencing the curse of this promise? Yet, following the war, after a huge sum was paid in reparation to the Jewish community, West Germany became the engine room of the European economy.

Was it Churchill's long standing support for the principle of a homeland for Jewish people and his public stand against the British Government over its proposals, in February 1939, that

Palestine should not become a Jewish State, despite the 1917 Balfour Declaration, that could be a factor in his emerging from the political wilderness to lead Britain as Prime Minister?

In 1945, how else does one explain, as hero of the War, that he should lose the election? Could it be that it was his part in covering up the knowledge, even by 1943, that Jews were being systematically exterminated in Europe, or his refusal to extend help to the shattered Jewish community in Britain, requested by the Chief Rabbi a matter of weeks before the election? In a similar way, was it his White Paper in 1922, responsible for ceding 76% of the British Mandate in Palestine ('I created Transjordan with the stroke of a pen on a Sunday afternoon in Cairo'), that was at the root of his political demise? For within weeks he had lost his seat in Parliament.

Does Harry Truman's astonishing victory over Thomas E. Dewey in November 1948 owe itself to God's blessing on a man who, as President of the USA, stunned the world by his prompt and surprise recognition of the State of Israel on May 14 1948, only moments after David Ben-Gurion's proclamation?

All this is speculative I know, but God is true to his word, even if other factors are at work as well. History bows the knee to the Lord Jesus Christ, and I have come to see that he remains covenanted to his promises to his people.

Did Stalin's sudden death on Thursday March 5 1953 have any connection with the arrest of nine eminent doctors at the beginning of that week, six of them Jewish, on a trumped up charge of plotting to kill political and military leaders, in order to release a wave of persecution of the Jews?

What of Anthony Eden in 1956 and his demise so soon after the debacle over the Suez affair? What of Ted Heath who refused to re-equip Israel with spares previously promised for armaments sold in the October 1973 Yom Kippur War? By December 17, Britain was on a three-day working week which forced Ted Heath into a General Election, which he lost.

What of Jim Callaghan's reneguing on an agreement to

supply Israel with oil after the Arab oil boycott? What of Margaret Thatcher, the longest serving Prime Minister and the first to visit Israel whilst in office? How was I to explain her eleven-year tenure? Could it be that as MP for Finchley, with its large Jewish population and her known support for Israel, that God honoured his promise?

This raises enormous questions, but God's word is the test, not political commentators. Her demise could possibly be linked to an increasingly sour relationship with Israel through successive ministers of her government. Did she tacitly accept British arms supply to Saddam Hussein, himself publicly promising to destroy Israel?

It was Friday April 2 1982. I well remember reading in *The Times* of Lord Carrington's visit to Israel as Foreign Secretary, with its main front page headline, 'Carrington sours Israel'. To everyone's surprise, on Monday April 5, Carrington resigned, accepting the 'responsibility for the very great national humiliation' of the invasion of the Falklands by Argentina. Was there a connection?

Again, my point is, not that I am getting any of these observations right but that what is right is seeking to see God's hand in history, and holding history up against his word. We learn, if we are willing to make mistakes as we grow.

What of Britain? Under a Queen (Victoria) who was warm towards Jewish people, we had a Jewish Prime Minister (and a Christian) in Benjamin Disraeli. We promised a homeland for the Jewish people in the famous Balfour Declaration of 1917. We had the greatest Empire the world had ever seen, but started to backtrack on our promises, both to the Jews and to the Arabs. (See Colin Chapman, *Whose Promised Land,* Lion: 1983, pp 54–59.) On July 24 1922, at the San Remo League of Nations Conference, we ceded 76% of the British Mandate to Transjordan, land that was promised under the Mandate to the Jews. It was in this year that the troubles in Ireland flared into such a problem that has been with us ever since. Then, as we actively resisted the return of the Jews, following the Second World War, we lost our Empire with hardly a fight.

Both the Ethiopian rebel armies, who were surrounding Addis Ababa in June 1991, and the remains of the Marxist Government of Ethiopia agreed to bless Israel by allowing 14,400 Ethiopian Jews to return to Israel in Operation Solomon. Did this have any connection with the fact that the moment the last had been airlifted out, the civil war ceased and the opposing factions made peace and formed a unity Government?

What is the situation in the United States at the time you read this? Historically, the United States has welcomed Jewish people to its shores and, more consistently than any other nation, affirmed the homeland for Jews. Has God blessed that nation in part for that reason?

What of George Bush, who was the most popular US president in modern history after the Gulf War? Yet, as soon as he opposed Israel over their need to absorb tens of thousands of returning Jews, especially Russian, through raising Home Loans guarantees, he became one of the most unpopular presidents in American history and lost the election.

Let me repeat that my point is not that these observations are necessarily correct. Some may be, or none. The point is that I believe that God does want us to see that he is sovereign in the affairs of our history. We lose the sense of awe if we think otherwise. More specifically, he will be true to his word.

The dates of the Jewish expulsions from different lands are well documented. (For example, Mattis, *The Jewish Time Line Encyclopaedia,* Jason Aronson: 1992.) Has the reader considered the cause/effect of the blessing (or otherwise) of those nations, cities and towns from which they were expelled? You imagine how our foreign policy, based as it is on self-interest, might be affected if this were demonstrably true. I am not wanting to propound a prosperity message, for blessing could well be in the sense of a flowering of the gospel and godliness.

Has God finished with Israel? Scripture replies categorically, 'God forbid!', 'By no means!' I sincerely believe that history proves that too, and we have not even considered whether the survival of Israel is not a miracle in itself.

'Can a mother forget the baby at her breast?'

If God has finished with Israel, then I now saw that his word would be meaningless. Like a nursing mother, God says, 'Though she may forget, I will not forget you! See, I have engraved you on the palms of my hands' (Isa 49:15, 16). That would certainly be one place where I would not want to be tattooed. How tender too are his words, 'for whoever touches you touches the apple of [my] eye' (Zech 2:8), the most sensitive part of our bodies. Yet it is to Israel that he speaks.

As a father, God says, 'Israel is my firstborn son' (Ex 4:22) and Israel responds, 'you, O Lord, are our Father' (Isa 63:16, 64:8; also Jer 3:19), the very words Jesus taught his disciples to pray, 'Our Father . . .'(Matt 6:9).

Isaiah 54 has the heading in the NIV, 'The future glory of Zion' and includes God's promise,

'For your Maker is your husband – the Lord Almighty is his name – the Holy One of Israel is your Redeemer . . .the Lord will call you back as if you were a wife deserted and distressed in spirit – a wife who married young' (54:5, 6).

God declares through Malachi (2:16) the simple words, 'I hate divorce'. Can he declare himself to be husband to Israel and then divorce her? Is the Church, the bride of Christ, that much more faithful? (Rev 21:2,9; 22:17). Are we 'without stain or wrinkle or any other blemish', are we 'holy and blameless' (Eph 5:27)?

Isaiah 54 continues,

> 'For a brief moment I abandoned you, but with deep compassion I will bring you back. In a surge of anger I hid my face from you for a moment, but with everlasting kindness I will have compassion on you, says the Lord your Redeemer (Isa 54:7, 8).

God likens that day to the days of Noah,

> 'when I swore that the waters of Noah would never again cover the earth. So now I have sworn not to be angry with you, never to rebuke you again. Though the mountains be shaken and the hills be removed, yet my unfailing love for you will not be shaken nor my covenant of peace be removed' (Isa 54:9–10).

As a kinsman redeemer, 'This is what the Lord says – Israel's King and Redeemer, the Lord Almighty: I am the first and I am the last . . .' (Isa 44:6); 'Remember these things, O Jacob, for you are my servant, O Israel . . . I will not forget you. I have swept away your offences like a cloud' (Isa 44:21–22). Jesus the Messiah is Israel's King and Redeemer, he is 'the First and the Last' (Rev 1:17).

'He who watches over Israel will neither slumber nor sleep' (Ps 121:4)

Has God finished with Israel? He would have to disown his very name to do so.

Chapter 18

THE FEAST OF TABERNACLES

I was quite content and relaxed in seeking to see God in the affairs of history. It is speculative, 'For we know in part and we prophesy in part' (1 Cor 13:9). There was still something missing in terms of linking prophecies yet to happen, and it was not until I had been thrown in the deep end that a crucial discovery took place.

I was asked to speak under the title, 'The Feast of Tabernacles, the future hope'. I had no idea what was expected and did not realise that I could be quite so excited by the discoveries I made!

Zechariah foretold that after the attack on Jerusalem by the all nations army, 'the survivors from all the nations that have attacked Jerusalem will go up year after year to worship the King, the Lord Almighty, and to celebrate the Feast of Tabernacles' (14:16). Here was the future hope but how was it possible to make sense of that?

First, a thumb nail sketch. The command to keep the Feast of Tabernacles, or the Feast of Booths or Shelters (Hebrew, sukkah = booth) is found in Leviticus 23:33–43, Dt 16:13–17. In Leviticus 23, God gave details of all the feasts that he called Israel to keep. 'These are my appointed feasts, the appointed feasts of the Lord' (23:2), Sabbath, Passover, Feast of Weeks

(Pentecost), Feast of Trumpets, Day of Atonement and the Feast of Tabernacles (the chapter is a positive goldmine!). In revealing how to keep them, God chose to create, within the different feasts, visual illustrations of the different doctrines concerning salvation history: rest at Sabbath to remember Creation; Passover to enact the Exodus; and so on.

Tabernacles was one of the three great pilgrimage festivals of the Jewish year (Dt 16:16). It occurs in October and lasts from the 15th to the 22nd of the seventh month of Tishri or Elthanor. During this time the people lived in temporary dwellings called booths. It would remind them of the frailty of their existence in the wilderness as wanderers. It was the only feast where it was commanded that they rejoice! (Lev 23:40).

The Feast celebrated God's redemption of Israel (23:43), his protection as they wandered in the wilderness, his guidance to the Promised Land and thanksgiving for the safe ingathering of the harvest (Dt 16:15). In Numbers 29:12–39 we are told that they were to sacrifice each day, and the rabbinic thinking is that these sacrifices represented the Gentile nations. So Israel, called to be a royal priesthood, was sacrificing on behalf of the Gentiles.

Tabernacles appears to have been a festival that expressed revival in Israel and a type of the final revival of all. The dedication of Solomon's Temple and revival of God's presence took place during the Feast of Tabernacles (2 Chron 5:3). It reminded them that their ancestors lived in tents and they could compare the transience of that journey with the permanence of the Temple. Solomon celebrated the Feast in the annual cycle of Feasts (2 Chron 8:13).

In the revival under Hezekiah, Tabernacles was kept (2 Chron 31:3) and when the exiles returned from Babylon under Zerubbabel (Ezra 3:4), they celebrated the Feast as prescribed in the Book of Moses (Neh 8:14–17).

Finally Jesus (Jn 7:2, 10–end) celebrated the Feast in Jerusalem. His brothers verbalised the Jewish belief that the

Messiah would reveal himself at Tabernacles in telling him that he should go up and reveal himself (7:3). It was in the context of the Festival that the question of his identity is set (7:25–31, 40–43). He stood up in the temple and proclaimed in a loud voice, 'If any man is thirsty, let him come to me and drink'(7:37) and the following day he said, 'I am the light of the world' (Jn 8:12). These three themes, namely the revelation of his true identity, and the images of water and light, are relevant to the hope of his future rule and reign.

It was so easy to overlook that there had been Messianic revival as Jesus' ministry began. 'The people were waiting *expectantly* and were all wondering in their hearts if John might possibly be the Christ' (Luke 3:15). At Jericho, after Zacchaeus had receieved Jesus, 'he went on to tell them a parable, because he was near Jerusalem and the people thought that the kingdom of God was going to appear *at once*' (Luke 19:11).

Five days before the Passover (Jn 12:12, see 12:1), it was a *great crowd* (a very large crowd, Matt 21:8) that had come for the Feast, that welcomed Jesus into Jerusalem. 'When Jesus entered Jerusalem, the whole city was stirred and asked, "Who is this?"' (Matt 21:10).

Following the raising of Lazarus, many people went out to meet him, 'So the Pharisees said to one another, "See, this is getting us nowhere. Look how *the whole world* has gone after him!"' (Jn 12:19) and 'What are we accomplishing? . . .Here is this man performing many miraculous signs. If we let him go on like this, everyone will believe in him' (Jn 11:47–48). 'But the chief priests, the teachers of the law and the leaders among the people were trying to kill him. Yet they could not find any way to do it, because *all* the people hung on his words' (Lk 19:47–48). 'Yet at the same time many even among the leaders believed in him. But because of the Pharisees they would not confess their faith for fear that they would be put out of the synagogue' (Jn 12:42).

Mark tells us that when the Passover was 'only two days away

. . . the chief priests and teachers of the law were looking for some sly way to arrest Jesus and kill him. "But not during the *Feast*," they said, "or the people may riot"' (Mk 14:1–2). Where the King is present, there the kingdom comes in power. Revival is a mark of Tabernacles.

Today, observant Jews will build their sukkah and celebrate for seven days with a special day at the end to rejoice in the law.

But what was the way to understand future hope?

The first principle had to be that Jesus fulfils Tabernacles. He had fulfilled Passover and becomes the Passover Lamb in his death, satisfying the Feast of Atonement. Paul said of the Communion, set in the context of a Passover meal, that 'whenever you eat this bread and drink this cup, you proclaim the Lord's death *until he comes*' (1 Cor 11:26). Passover therefore no longer has a purpose once Jesus comes again. As we have seen, the Feast of Weeks (Pentecost or firstfruits – Ex 34:22) was fulfilled on the very day he sent the Holy Spirit on the firstfruits of those redeemed. Through his resurrection he was 'the firstfruits of those who have fallen asleep'(1 Cor 15:20, 23) and in the sending of the Holy Spirit, 'we ourselves. . .have the first- fruits of the Spirit' (Rom 8:23).

But in what way does Jesus fulfil the Feast of Tabernacles?

1. Did Jesus come at Tabernacles?

Though there is no way that I can prove it, and the evidence is tenuous, I believe that Jesus could very well have been born at Tabernacles. Clearly it was not at Christmas that he was born, as the shepherds and sheep could well have frozen to death. However cruel the Romans may have been, there would be no way they could organise a census in the middle of winter (Lk 2:4–5)! The only alternative was that he was born at a random date, yet he fulfils so completely Passover and Pentecost, that this made no sense to me.

If there are any clues, the first may be that Luke is careful to record the timing of events. 'In the sixth month, God sent the angel Gabriel to Nazareth, a town in Galilee, to a virgin pledged to be married to a man named Joseph, a descendant of David' (Lk 1:26–27). The time span is six months after the angel of the Lord visited Zechariah in the Temple (Lk 1:5–22). He was on duty serving as a priest. Luke tells us that he is of the house of Abijah (Lk 1:5) and the NIV gives a cross reference to 1 Chronicles 24:10, that lists the order in which the priestly divisions serve in the Temple. There are twenty-four, just as there are twenty-four elders around the throne of God (Rev 4:4). Zechariah's division was eighth in the rota. Does that makes his division's turn on the rota the second half of the fourth month? I thought it was only the Church of England that ran on rotas!

Were the rota to begin with the start of the Jewish religious New Year which began with Passover (Ex 12:2) in the month of Abib, or Nisan, this would correspond with our March or April. If in the year that Jesus was born, Passover fell in our March, then, according to the rota, Zechariah might well have been in the Temple sixteen weeks later, in the second half of (our) June. Six months later (Lk 1:26), when Gabriel visits Mary, would bring us to the second half of our December.

The Eastern Orthodox Church celebrates our Christmas as the Feast of the Conception, as they believe that this was when Jesus was conceived and that it was in the second half of our December that the angel Gabriel spoke to Mary. That certainly fits with this possibility that Zechariah was in the temple in June. Nine months of pregnancy from December would take us into September and that is around the time of Tabernacles! Could this be why John says, 'The Word became flesh and tabernacled among us' (Jn 1:14. Bagster, *The Englishman's Greek New Testament*)? Interestingly, the Hebrew for stable, where, traditionally, we see Jesus born, is *sukkah*, or shelter, or tabernacle (Gen 33:17 and NIV footnote). Was it a stable where Jesus was born, or was it within the sukkah, or shelter, constructed for the Feast of Tabernacles?

Yes, this is speculative, but it attempts to honour the precision with which Jesus came 'to fulfil the Law and the Prophets' (Matt 5:17).

If this is part of the fulfilment, it was hidden from the world, just as he hid himself from revealing who he was at the Feast in Jerusalem.

2. He fulfils the themes of Tabernacles

We have seen that the Jews expected the Messiah to reveal himself at Tabernacles and this may explain the curious response by Peter as he sees the Messiah in his glory on the Mount of Transfiguration, 'Let us put up three shelters – one for you, one for Moses and one for Elijah' (Lk 9:33). He did not know what he was saying, but his immediate reaction was to build a booth or shelter as he would at Tabernacles, for there in front of him was the glorified Messiah!

Secondly, Jesus fulfils the meaning of the themes that make up Tabernacles, redemption, protection, guidance in the wilderness, and (a later addition) the provision of water and the lighting of four huge candelabra in the Temple court that lit up the whole of Jerusalem.

3. Will Jesus come again at Tabernacles?

My conviction is that Jesus will return at Tabernacles, albeit that we do not know the day or the hour. Zechariah 14:4 says that Jesus comes to the Mount of Olives (Acts 1:11). When Jesus wept over Jerusalem, he said, 'For I tell you, you will not see me again until you say, "Blessed is he who comes in the name of the Lord"' (Matt 23:39). He is quoting Psalm 118:26, one of the Hallel Psalms, a psalm about national salvation and one of the praise psalms quoted at Tabernacles.

All the other festivals will have found their fulfilment whereas Jesus fulfils the themes of Tabernacles in his future reign.

Apart from the Lamentations of Jeremiah, all the prophets have passages of restoration that shine like rays of sunshine out of the dark skies of judgment. To my amazement so many of them fell into the categories of the themes of Tabernacles.

For instance, Tabernacles remains a pilgrimage feast and a celebration, for '. . . the nations will go up year after year [to Jerusalem] to worship the King, the Lord Almighty, and to celebrate the Feast of Tabernacles' (Zech 14:16). It celebrates the ingathering of the harvest. This is the only festival to which Gentiles are commanded to come (14:17), and a theme of Tabernacles is rejoicing at the ingathering of the harvest amongst the Gentiles.

In the same way as the booths or shelters have to be constructed so as to be open to the sky, Jesus said, 'When these things begin to take place, stand up and lift up your heads, because your redemption is drawing near' (Lk 21:28). We are called to look up. It is from the sky that Jesus will appear (Acts 1:11), 'Look, he is coming with the clouds, and every eye will see him, even those who pierced him' (Rev 1:7). We have already seen that 'those who pierced him' refers to Zechariah 12:10, 'They will look on me, the one they have pierced.' Has God finished with Israel? How could he, for he returns in such a manner that Israel sees him and mourns for him 'as one mourns for an only child'.

Light is a theme of Tabernacles, and at his return we are told, 'On that day there will be no light, no cold or frost. It will be a unique day, without daytime and night-time – a day known to the Lord. When evening comes, there will be light' (Zech 14:6–7). Jesus is the 'light of the world'(Jn 8:12).

Thanksgiving for the provision of rain was celebrated. The booths were open to the sky so that rain might be felt. At the feast, a ceremony of thanksgiving for water takes place, where the priests process to the Pool of Siloam and return to the Temple to pour out the water over the altar. So it is the withholding of rain that is the subject of judgment upon nations that do not go up to the feast (Zech 14:17–18). Furthermore, 'On that day living water will flow out from Jerusalem, half to the eastern sea and half to the western sea [Dead Sea and Mediterranean – NIV footnote], in summer and in winter' (Zech 14:8). In the same way as the floodwaters covered the earth, so, 'the earth will be filled with the knowledge of the glory of the Lord, as the waters cover the sea' (Hab 2:14, cf Isa 11:9). It was at the Feast that Jesus promised that 'streams of living water' would flow from within those who were spiritually thirsty and who came to him to drink (Jn 7:37–38).

Yes, I know that all these verses raise masses of questions, but that is no bad thing. The point is that it is the Feast of Tabernacles that holds together these different themes, and it is these themes that can be found in so many of the passages of Scripture that allude to a millennial, earthly reign. By saying that the Church has replaced Israel, we have nowhere to place these Scriptures except to spiritualise them. They simply do not fit.

Tabernacles is a time of eating meals outside in the sukkah, and Jesus refers to a future time when he will eat and drink with his disciples (Matt 26:29). Isaiah speaks of a future meal, 'On this mountain the Lord Almighty will prepare a feast of rich food for all peoples ['peoples', plural, refers to Gentiles], a banquet of aged wine – the best of meats and the finest of wines' (Isa 25:6). Jesus had said to his disciples, in the context of his return, 'like men waiting for their master to return . . .he will dress himself to serve, will have them recline at the table and will come and wait on them' (Lk 12:36–37). I had seen this to be in heaven, but there were too many passages that could only find fulfilment in an earthly period of the reign and rule of the King in Scripture that simply did not fit with an abrupt end to the world and then heaven or hell!

Rejoicing in the law (Simchat Torah) is an integral part of Tabernacles, and the prophets say of the law,

Many peoples will come and say, 'Come let us go up to the mountain of the Lord, to the house of the God of Jacob. He will teach us
his ways, so that we may walk in his paths.' The law will go out from
Zion, the word of the Lord from Jerusalem (Isa 2:3, Mic 4:2).

We have seen how God's protection enabled the Children of
Israel to enter the Promised Land. The heart of the Feast still
remains redemption and God's protection. No more the protection in the wilderness from the harshness of the desert, but protection in a planet that without the return of the Maker of
heaven and earth, we would have destroyed ourselves. In
response to the disciples' asking, 'What will be the sign of your
coming and of the end of the age?' (Matt 24:3), Jesus said that
there would be days of great and unequalled distress, and 'if
those days had not been cut short, no-one would survive'
(24:21–22). Now, the Lord destroys the very things that
threaten all of us,

He will judge between many peoples and will settle disputes for
strong nations far and wide. They will beat their swords into
ploughshares and their spears into pruning hooks. Nation will not
take up sword against nation, nor will they train for war any more'
(Mic 4:3, cf Isa 2:4).

How were this agricultural people to know that war and the
armaments industry would be the threat of world destruction?
How wonderful that the Messiah can disarm nations! 'For he
must reign until he has put all his enemies under his feet. The
last enemy to be destroyed is death' (1 Cor 15:25–26).

Yes, I believe these prophecies are referring to the future
Feast of Tabernacles that brings together these different
themes. Tabernacles fits such a kingly rule and reign. I can only
suggest that this be taken, again, as a hypothesis and then be
tested by the reader.

Chapter 19

THE BOOK OF REVELATION

We have seen how the prophets tell of Jesus' coming with such amazing accuracy. We have seen the prophecies that Jesus gave concerning his Second Coming and the signs of the times. We have looked at signs of the restoration of Israel from the Hebrew prophets. We are still testing the theory that God has *not* finished with Israel.

I had a conviction by now that the gospels, Acts and the letters all supported the theory, but what of the last book of the Bible? It would be impossible to give a brief synopsis of Revelation as a whole, but is Israel forgotten?

The Revelation is of Jesus. In chapter one, 'Look, he is coming with the clouds, and every eye will see him, even those who pierced him . . .' (Rev 1:7). This is cross referenced to Zechariah 12:10, 'those who pierced him' referring to the Jewish people of whom, when they are back in their land, as Zechariah foretold 'will look on me the one they have pierced' (12:10).

'His head and hair were white like wool, as white as snow, and his eyes were like blazing fire' (Rev 1:14), just as Daniel had seen (Dan 7:9), affirming the prophet. Revelation 2:27 is a quotation from Psalm 2:9, which also speaks of Jesus thus, 'I have installed my King on Zion, my holy hill' (2:6). Jesus is the one 'who holds the key of David' (Rev 3:7).

'Surrounding the throne were. . . twenty-four elders' (Rev 4:4). Jesus had already said that the apostles would sit on twelve thrones (Matt 19:28), so do we not see here a picture of the Church and the twelve tribes of Israel united under an eldership?

Jesus is described as 'the Lion of the tribe of Judah, the Root of David' (Rev 5:5), titles that speak of a continuity with Israel. From all the tribes of Israel, we read of 144,000 who were sealed, with the names of the tribes specifically mentioned (Rev 7:4–8).

The Hebrew language is still considered relevant. The writer translates the name of the angel of the abyss into Hebrew and Greek (Rev 9:11), and Armageddon is described as being a Hebrew word (Rev 16:16).

In the vision of the angel and the little scroll in Revelation 10, the angel announces, 'the mystery of God will be accomplished, just as he announced to his servants the prophets' (10:7). He affirms that there is no discontinuity between what was foretold by the prophets and what is to come.

The 'holy city' is mentioned in chapter 11:2, and in chapter 12 the vision of the 'woman and the dragon' also appears to speak of Israel. The woman gives 'birth to a son, a male child, who will rule all the nations with an iron sceptre. And her child was snatched up to God and to his throne' (12:5). That surely speaks of Jesus, ascended, and to rule the nations. Israel fits the picture of the woman in the vision, and there could be a cross reference to Isaiah 66:7–9.

In Chapter 14, we are given the picture of 'the Lamb, standing on Mount Zion, and with him 144,000 . . .' (14:1 and cross reference to 7:4 mentioned above). In Chapter 15 reference is made to them singing 'the song of Moses the servant of God . . .' (15:3).

It is perhaps worth mentioning the problem that references to the Temple create in Revelation. It is not my purpose to try and explain Revelation, but merely to show that there is still a close correlation with the revelation of what is to come and things identifiably related with Israel. The temple is mentioned in 3:12, 7:15, 11:1, 2(AV), 11:19 (twice), 14:15, 17, 15:5, 6, 8 (twice);16:1, 17 and 21:22 (twice). The latter indicates that John 'did not see a temple in the city,' whereas the rest indicate that he did (I am so glad that this is not a book on how to understand Revelation!).

To return to the theme of seeing in Revelation aspects that speak of Israel,

> After this I looked and in heaven the temple, that is, the tabernacle of the Testimony, was opened. Out of the temple came the seven angels . . . And the temple was filled with smoke from the glory of God . . .and no-one could enter the temple. . . (15:5–8).

One cannot help but be reminded of the dedication of the temple by Solomon, 'Then the temple of the Lord was filled with a cloud, and the priests could not perform their service because of the cloud, for the glory of the Lord filled the temple of God' (2 Chron 5:13b–14).

In Revelation 16:15 we read, 'Behold, I come like a thief', and we have seen that Jesus spoke similar words to his disciples (Lk 12:39–40). The very next verse (Rev 16:16) says, 'Then they gathered the kings together to the place that in Hebrew is called Armageddon.' Books have been written about that! Here we are simply noting the link that Revelation has with the land of Israel. Armageddon is at present-day Megiddo in the vicinity of the Carmel range.

Chapter 19 describes that paean of praise, 'Hallelujah! For our Lord God Almighty reigns' (Rev 19:6). Israel too is connected with God's title, Almighty. The Greek word is *pantokrator* and means 'ruler of all'. The word is introduced in the Septuagint as a translation of 'Lord [or God] of hosts' (see Jer 5:14, Amos 3:13).

I was staggered to read in the Preface to the NIV, the following,

Because for most readers today the phrases 'the Lord of hosts' and 'God of hosts' have little meaning, this version renders them 'the Lord Almighty' and 'God Almighty'. These renderings convey the sense of the Hebrew, namely, 'he who is sovereign over all the "hosts" (powers) in heaven and on earth, especially over the "hosts" (armies) *of Israel*.'

Ponder a moment on that last sentence, 'especially over the "hosts" (armies) of Israel.' Does the title 'Lord Almighty' convey that sense or have we lost something in the translation, particularly relating to Israel? Is God *still* sovereign over the hosts (armies) of Israel? But we must press on.

Chapter 20 speaks of the thousand year period when Satan is bound (20:2) and released (20:7), it foretells of an army that 'marched across the breadth of the earth and surrounded the camp of God's people, the city he loves' (20:9), which is referring to the prophecy of Ezekiel,

> In that day, when my people Israel are living in safety, will you not take notice of it? You will come from your place in the far north, you and many nations with you . . . You will advance against my people Israel like a cloud that covers the land. In days to come, O Gog, I will bring you against my land, so that the nations may know me when I show myself holy through you (Ezek 38:14–16).

We read of books being opened (Rev 20:12, 15), the books pictured in the vision that Daniel received at night, 'the court was seated and the books were opened' (Dan 7:10).

As the book of Revelation reaches its climax, we read of 'the Holy City, the new Jerusalem, coming down out of heaven from God, prepared as a bride beautifully dressed for her husband' (21:2 and also 10). Imagery that speaks of a continuing relationship with Israel. The walls and gates of the Holy City are mentioned, 'On the gates were written the names of the twelve tribes of Israel' (21:12) and 'The wall of the city had twelve foundations, and on them were the names of the twelve apostles of the Lamb' (21:14).

The message concludes, 'I, Jesus, have sent my angel to give you this testimony for the churches. I am the Root and the Offspring of David' (22:16). The holy city is referred to in verse 19, and the book ends with 'The grace of the Lord Jesus be with God's people. Amen' (22:21), the term 'people' being the very description that is consistently given for the people of Israel in the Hebrew Scriptures, into whom we Gentiles are grafted. 'Amen' is a Hebrew word from the root meaning 'to be firm, steady and trustworthy' – in fact the very name of Jesus, as he introduces himself in the letter to the church in Laodicea, 'These are the words of the Amen, the faithful and true witness, the ruler of God's creation' (3:14), whose name in Hebrew is *Yeshua Ha'Mashiach*.

Even Revelation, for all the difficulties that it raises, assumes, as do the covenants, that the *People* and the *Place*, that is the land of Israel, are to be an integral part of the final bringing together of Jews and Gentiles. Furthermore, the *Purpose* that all peoples will be blessed (Gen 12:3) will be fulfilled when there is 'a great multitude that no-one [can] count, from every nation, tribe, people and language, standing before the throne and in front of the Lamb' (Rev 7:9). The final element of the covenants, namely that the promises will be fulfilled *in Perpetuity*, is gloriously encompassed in the angelic host's worshipping God, saying 'Amen! Praise and glory and wisdom and thanks and honour and power and strength be to our God *for ever and ever*. Amen!' (Rev 7:12). The blessing promised to all who will receive is that 'they will reign *for ever and ever*' (Rev 22:5b) – *in Perpetuity* make!

Chapter 20

WHERE DO WE GO FROM HERE?

May I leave you with a few practical thoughts? The content of this book has taken the author some considerable time to digest and may have left the reader with more questions than answers! I would merely ask that the question of God's purpose for Israel be not forgotten in the rush of so many other issues facing the Church. On this issue, like every other, we have to 'continue to work out [our] salvation with fear and trembling' (Phil 2:12).

Resolving our differences

There are very real differences that this subject creates. How might we handle our differing opinions? Some suggestions:

a) Our commitment is first and foremost to our Lord Jesus Christ, and we need constantly to make sure that our views on Israel and the end times are firmly placed in submission to him. All that has been written pales into insignificance when compared with the saving love of God in Christ Jesus.

b) We are commanded to love one another. Even if ideologically we are in different camps, nonetheless we are required to follow that way of love (Matt 5:43).

c) If someone takes an opposing view to yourself, take time to understand how that person got to that place.

d) We are to pray for unity. God our Father will never fail to hear the prayer deep in the heart of his Son that we may be one (Jn 17:21–23). That prayer foresaw the enormous gulf between Jew and Gentile. Divisions over eschatology (end times) are fairly minor by comparison!

e) Meet with those of opposing views. As someone once wrote 'mud thrown is ground lost'.

f) Acknowledge that there is division and that it is painful to the body of Christ. We need to repent of our divisions and the hardness of heart this causes. Forgive where forgiveness is needed.

g) Listen to opposing views to your own and make sure that you listen carefully, for language can have different interpretations. Be willing to have your views tested.

h) Allow the views of others to be an incentive to go back to Scripture. If that differing view is found to be correct then you have gained. If it is not, then further study will deepen your conviction.

i) Interpretation of Biblical prophecy must submit to sound exegetical principles. Beware of merely picking on a few favourite verses and ignoring others that don't suit your argument!

j) Think through together the outworking of your different conclusions. They may even lead to creative applications that actually complement one another.

Some conclusions

a) See Jewish people in a new light. You may know Jewish people, you may work with them or have Jewish neighbours. See them as 'loved on account of the patriarchs' (Rom 11:28).

b) Above all, pray for Israel and the Jewish people. Pray for an understanding of God's purposes for the Jewish people. If Paul concludes his teaching in Romans concerning God's future purposes for Israel with the doxology, 'Oh, the depths of the riches of the wisdom and knowledge of God!' (Rom 11:33), then let's pray for that wisdom and knowledge!

Pray that we might love Jewish people, for if we have received God's love 'poured. . .into our hearts by the Holy Spirit, whom he has given us' (Rom 5:5), then, because 'they are loved on account of the patriarchs,' his love for his covenanted people can become ours.

'Pray for the peace of Jerusalem' (Ps 122:6). That will mean praying for a very complex network of issues. There is tremendous conflict, and great wisdom and grace is needed.

c) Appreciate our debt to Israel. They were the receivers of God's word, they are the people from whom our Messiah comes, and from them we Gentiles first heard the gospel. Their Saviour has become ours (Rom 9:4–5). Their Scriptures reveal our salvation. The price of their hardness enabled our salvation (Rom 11:12, 25).

d) Find ways of involving your church to better understand God's plan for Israel. It may be by having a Passover meal together, leading up to Easter. It may be through studying this subject in a home group. It may be by asking the minister to consider giving some teaching on the subject. If the church is to rely on 'the nourishing sap from the olive root' (Rom 11:17), what a tragedy it would be if we lost the very source of that sap.

Paul warns the church of boasting (Rom 11:18), arrogance (11:20), ignorance (11:25) and conceit (11:25). Discern what is the theological basis of a preacher or teacher's interpretation of Scripture. Has the assumption been made that Israel has been rejected?

Consider the words of our hymns, choruses and spiritual songs. Have we replaced Israel and transferred all the promises to the Church? Then there will be strange lack of witness by the Holy Spirit. We will be singing about the land of Israel as though it is ours!

e) Within your planned giving, choose to return a blessing to those involved in a ministry of love and care for Jewish people. Paul concludes his teaching in Romans by saying, 'For if the Gentiles have shared in the Jews' spiritual blessings, they owe it to the Jews to share with them their material blessings' (Rom 15:27).

f) Encourage Messianic believers in the Lord Jesus Christ. They can easily be misunderstood by the church in that they are working out for themselves what true Jewishness means, and that is a process that takes time. They are ostracised by their own community and thus are caught between both the church and the synagogue.

g) Repent of any attitudes and actions that are anti-Semitic. Has there been past persecution by your family, church, district or nation that needs confession and repentance?

h) Support the work of sharing the love of Yeshua among Jewish people. 'How, then, can they call on the one they have not believed in? And how can they believe in the one of whom they have not heard? And how can they hear without someone preaching to them?' (Rom 10:14). Paul certainly does not give us ground to argue that a future sovereign ingathering means that until then, we leave Jewish people well alone as far as the gospel is concerned. Is the gospel 'good news'? Then what is it saying of the Church if good news is withheld from anyone?

It is my conviction that because we have forgotten this priority, the church has lost a central focus of unity. The commitment to go 'first to the Jew' was one of the church's earliest convictions, and I believe that this is one significant reason why the church has splintered over every other conceivable issue into well over 20,000 denominations. We have lost our evangelistic zeal. Yes, it is a sensitive issue, given the appalling record of Christian anti-Semitism over the past 2,000 years, but if the gospel is not to be preached to Jewish people, then why to any other ethnic group or nation?

'You who bring good tidings to Zion. . .lift up your voice with a shout, lift it up, do not be afraid; say to the towns of Judah, "Here is your God!"' (Isa 40:9). His name is Jesus, *Yeshua Ha'Mashiach.*

i) Search the Scriptures daily to see if these things are so (Acts 17:11). This is only one man's search, and all of us are challenged 'to work out [our] salvation with fear and trembling, for it is God who works in [us]' (Phil 2:12–13). For me, the place of Israel in God's purpose integrates both the Hebrew Scriptures and New Testament, it helps explain aspects of nations and history, it is a factor in understanding present day events in the world, and crucial as far as the Middle East is concerned, not to mention being central to the Coming of the Lord Jesus Christ. There cannot be many issues that have such far-reaching significance.

For God has spoken,

'I will make you into a great nation and I will bless you; I will make your name great, and you will be a blessing. I will bless those who bless you, and whoever curses you I will curse; and all peoples on earth will be blessed through you' (Gen 12:2, 3).

In closing, 'May the God of hope fill you with all joy and peace as you trust in him, so that you may overflow with hope by the power of the Holy Spirit' (Rom 15:13), and 'The Lord bless you and keep you; the Lord make his face shine upon you and be gracious to you; the Lord turn his face towards you and give you peace' (Num 6:24–26).

'The glory of the Lord will be revealed, and all mankind together will see it' (Isa 40:5).

Appendix 1

A SUGGESTED COLOUR CODING

The following are only *suggested* ways in which we might mark our Bibles. I use 'Stabiloboss Dry' wax crayons made by Schwan. They are highlight colours, but the joy is that they can be erased if a mistake is made, and they do not show through the paper!

Themes and their colours

RED	Sin, judgment and redemption (cross, blood, etc.)
BLUE	The titles of Jesus in both the Hebrew Scriptures and the New Testament
GREEN	Israel, the land, the law and Hebrew/Jewish issues
YELLOW	Prophecy
ORANGE	Miracles (signs and wonders), including fulfilled prophecy and references to the Holy Spirit

I do not have colours for God the Father.

Themes and their underlinings

I use fine line ball-point pens to *underline* the following:

GREEN   Gentiles (In the OT = nations/peoples)
RED   God's covenant promises
BLUE   Mankind's response in obedience to God

That still leaves black. You may prefer to include passages of a devotional nature and reserve one of these colours for that.

If you are using a wide margined Study Bible, then different ball-point colours can help in making margin notes: viz, blue or black for headings, and the others for margin comments. Where two or three different margin comments are made alongside one verse, then using different colours for each thought helps to differentiate them. If the comment is too long for the margin, then a footnote number can be given and then written on the bottom or top margin of the page. If I do make a mistake, or want to erase a comment, then Tippex fluid works well.

Finally, if a useful quotation, margin note or summary on any theme is not to be 'lost', then a verse reference (or page and footnote number) against the key word can be written in the Concordance at the back, to indicate that you have a worthwhile reference on that theme.

Appendix 2

SCRIPTURE REFERENCES

USEFUL WEBSITES

www.ravello.co.uk/olive-tree

www.premieronline.co.uk